CHRIST AND HIS RIGHTEOUSNESS

BY E. J. WAGGONER.

"And this is his name whereby he shall be called, THE LORD OUR RIGHTEOUSNESS." Jer. 23:6.

"But of Him are ye in Christ Jesus, who of God is made unto us wisdom, and righteousness, and sanctification, and redemption." I Cor. 1:30.

Upward Way

Pioneer Classics

1st EDITION–1988
2nd EDITION–1990
3rd EDITION–1992
COPYRIGHT © 1992
UPWARD WAY, INC.
P.O. BOX 369
PLEASANT VIEW, TN 37146
(800) 367-2665
Printed In U.S.A.
ISBN 0-945460-01-5

CHRIST AND HIS
RIGHTEOUSNESS

Contents

Choice
Reading

from Upward Way, Inc.
or your local Christian bookstore

CHRIST
AND HIS RIGHTEOUSNESS

by E. J. Waggoner

A precious treasure waiting to be discovered by the present generation, this book is a breakthrough. It penetrates centuries of spiritual fog to rediscover the inherent power of pure New Testament justification by faith. The author demonstrates how to overcome that all-too-common sinful paralysis—by believing how good the Good News is.

96 pages

THE CONSECRATED WAY

by Alonzo T. Jones

A contemporary of E.J. Waggoner. Strongly recommended as excellent companion reading with CHRIST and HIS RIGHTEOUSNESS. Focusing on Christ's work in the Heavenly Sanctuary, this book is a study in the books of Daniel and Hebrews. Christ is uplifted as our Example, Saviour, Mediator, and King. *96 pages*

FOR QUANTITY ORDERS:

Contact your local Christian bookstore or Upward Way, Inc. at 1-800-367-2665.

CHRIST

AND

HIS RIGHTEOUSNESS.

In the first verse of the third chapter of Hebrews we have an exhortation which comprehends all the injunctions given to the Christian. It is this: "Wherefore, holy brethren, partakers of the heavenly calling, consider the Apostle and High Priest of our profession, Christ Jesus." To do this as the Bible enjoins, to consider Christ continually and intelligently, just as He is, will transform one into a perfect Christian, for "by beholding we become changed."

Ministers of the Gospel have an inspired warrant for keeping the theme, Christ, continually before the people, and directing the attention of the people to Him alone. Paul said to the Corinthians, "I determined not to know anything among you, save Jesus Christ, and Him crucified" (1 Cor. 2:2); and there is no reason to suppose that his preaching to the Corinthians was different in any respect from his preaching elsewhere. Indeed, he tells us that when God revealed His Son in him, it was that he

might preach Him among the heathen (Gal. 1 : 15,
16); and his joy was that to him grace had been
given to "preach among the Gentiles the unsearch-
able riches of Christ." Eph. 3 : 8.

But the fact that the apostles made Christ the
burden of all their preaching, is not our sole warrant for magnifying Him. His Name is the only
name under heaven given among men whereby we
can be saved. Acts 4: 12. Christ Himself declared
that no man can come unto the Father but by Him.
John 14: 6. To Nicodemus He said: "And as Moses lifted up the serpent in the wilderness, even so
must the Son of Man be lifted up; that whosoever
believeth in Him should not perish, but have eternal
life." John 3 : 14, 15. This "lifting up" of Jesus,
while it has primary reference to His crucifixion,
embraces more than the mere historical fact; it
means that Christ must be "lifted up" by all who
believe in Him, as the crucified Redeemer, whose
grace and glory are sufficient to supply the world's
greatest need; it means that He should be "lifted
up" in all His exceeding loveliness and power as
"God with us," that His Divine attractiveness may
thus draw all unto Him. See John 12 : 32.

The exhortation to consider Jesus, and also the
reason therefor, are given in Heb. 12: 1–3: "Wherefore seeing we also are compassed about with so
great a cloud of witnesses, let us lay aside every
weight, and the sin which doth so easily beset us,
and let us run with patience the race that is set be-

fore us, looking unto Jesus the Author and Finisher of our faith; who for the joy that was set before Him endured the cross, despising the shame, and is set down at the right hand of the throne of God. For consider Him that endured such contradiction of sinners against Himself, lest ye be wearied and faint in your minds." It is only by constantly and prayerfully considering Jesus as He is revealed in the Bible, that we can keep from becoming weary in well-doing, and from fainting by the way.

Again, we should consider Jesus because in Him "are hid all the treasures of wisdom and knowledge." Col. 2 : 3. Whoever lacks wisdom is directed to ask of God, who gives to all men liberally and upbraids not, and the promise is that it shall be given him; but the desired wisdom can be obtained only in Christ. The wisdom which does not proceed from Christ, and which does not as a consequence lead to Him, is only foolishness; for God, as the Source of all things, is the Author of wisdom; ignorance of God is the worst sort of foolishness (see Rom. 1 : 21, 22); and all the treasures of wisdom and knowledge are hid in Christ; so that he who has only the wisdom of this world knows, in reality, nothing. And since all power in heaven and in earth is given to Christ, the apostle Paul declares Christ to be "the power of God, and the wisdom of God." 1 Cor. 1 : 24.

There is one text, however, which briefly sums up all that Christ is to man, and gives the most

comprehensive reason for considering Him. It is
this: "But of Him are ye in Christ Jesus, who of
God is made unto us wisdom, and righteousness,
and sanctification, and redemption." 1 Cor. 1 : 30.
We are ignorant, wicked, lost; Christ is to us wisdom, righteousness, redemption. What a range!
From ignorance and sin to righteousness and redemption. Man's highest aspiration or need cannot reach outside the bounds of what Christ is to
us, and of what He alone is to us. Sufficient reason
this why the eyes of all should be fixed upon Him.

HOW SHALL WE CONSIDER CHRIST?

But *how* should we consider Christ?—Just as He
has revealed Himself to the world; according to the
witness which He bore concerning Himself. In that
marvelous discourse recorded in the fifth chapter of
John, Jesus said: "For as the Father raiseth up the
dead, and quickeneth them; even so the Son quickeneth whom He will. For the Father judgeth no
man, but hath committed all judgment unto the
Son; that all men should honor the Son, even as
they honor the Father. He that honoreth not the
Son honoreth not the Father which hath sent Him."
Verses 21–23.

To Christ is committed the highest prerogative,
that of judging. He must receive the same honor
that is due to God, and for the reason that He is
God. The beloved disciple bears this witness: "In
the beginning was the Word, and the Word was

with God, and the Word was God." John 1:1. That this Divine Word is none other than Jesus Christ is shown by verse 14: "And the Word was made flesh, and dwelt among us (and we beheld His glory, the glory as of the Only-begotten of the Father), full of grace and truth."

The Word was "in the beginning." The mind of man cannot grasp the ages that are spanned in this phrase. It is not given to men to know when or how the Son was begotten; but we know that He was the Divine Word, not simply before He came to this earth to die, but even before the world was created. Just before His crucifixion He prayed, "And now, O Father, glorify thou Me with Thine own self with the glory which I had with Thee before the world was." John 17:5. And more than seven hundred years before His first advent, His coming was thus foretold by the word of inspiration: "But thou, Bethlehem Ephratah, though thou be little among the thousands of Judah, yet out of thee shall He come forth unto Me that is to be ruler in Israel; whose goings forth have been from of old, from the days of eternity." Micah 5:2, margin. We know that Christ "proceeded forth and came from God" (John 8:42), but it was so far back in the ages of eternity as to be far beyond the grasp of the mind of man.

IS CHRIST GOD?

In many places in the Bible Christ is called God. The Psalmist says: "The mighty God, even the

Lord [Jehovah], hath spoken, and called the earth from the rising of the sun unto the going down thereof. Out of Zion, the perfection of beauty, God hath shined. Our God shall come, and shall not keep silence; a fire shall devour before Him, and it shall be very tempestuous round about Him. He shall call to the heavens from above, and to the earth, that He may judge His people. Gather My saints together unto Me; those that have made a covenant with Me by sacrifice. And the heavens shall declare His righteousness; for God is judge Himself." Ps. 50: 1–6.

That this passage has reference to Christ may be known (1) by the fact already learned, that all judgment is committed to the Son; and (2) by the fact that it is at the second coming of Christ that He sends His angels to gather together His elect from the four winds. Matt. 24:31. "Our God shall come, and shall not keep silence." No; for when the Lord Himself descends from heaven, it will be " with a shout, with the voice of the archangel, and with the trump of God." 1 Thess. 4:16. This shout will be the voice of the Son of God, which will be heard by all that are in their graves, and which will cause them to come forth. John 5:28, 29. With the living righteous they will be caught up to meet the Lord in the air, ever more to be with Him; and this will constitute "our gathering together unto Him." 2 Thess. 2:1. Compare Ps. 50:5; Matt. 24: 31, and 1 Thess. 4: 16.

"A fire shall devour before Him, and it shall be very tempestuous round about Him;" for when the Lord Jesus shall be revealed from heaven with His mighty angels, it will be "in flaming fire taking vengeance on them that know not God, and that obey not the Gospel of our Lord Jesus Christ." 2 Thess. 1 : 8. So we know that Ps. 50: 1–6 is a vivid description of the second coming of Christ for the salvation of His people. When He comes it will be as "the mighty God." Compare Habakkuk 3.

This is one of His rightful titles. Long before Christ's first advent, the prophet Isaiah spoke these words of comfort to Israel: "For unto us a Child is born, unto us a Son is given; and the government shall be upon His shoulder; and His name shall be called Wonderful, Counselor, the mighty God, the everlasting Father, the Prince of Peace." Isa. 9:6.

These are not simply the words of Isaiah; they are the words of the Spirit of God. God has, in direct address to the Son, called Him by the same title. In Ps. 45:6 we read these words: "Thy throne, O God, is forever and ever; the scepter of Thy kingdom is a right scepter." The casual reader might take this to be simply the Psalmist's ascription of praise to God; but when we turn to the New Testament, we find that it is much more. We find that God the Father is the speaker, and that he is addressing the Son, calling Him God. See Heb. 1: 1–8.

This name was not given to Christ in consequence of some great achievement, but it is His by right of inheritance. Speaking of the power and greatness of Christ, the writer to the Hebrews says that He is made so much better than the angels, because "He hath *by inheritance* obtained a more excellent name than they." Heb. 1 :4. A son always rightfully takes the name of the father; and Christ, as "the only-begotten Son of God," has rightfully the same name. A son, also, is, to a greater or less degree, a reproduction of the father; he has, to some extent, the features and personal characteristics of his father; not perfectly, because there is no perfect reproduction among mankind. But there is no imperfection in God, or in any of His works; and so Christ is the "express image" of the Father's person. Heb. 1:3. As the Son of the self-existent God, he has by nature all the attributes of Deity.

It is true that there are many sons of God; but Christ is the "only-begotten Son of God," and therefore the Son of God in a sense in which no other being ever was, or ever can be. The angels are sons of God, as was Adam (Job 38:7; Luke 3:38), by creation; Christians are the sons of God by adoption (Rom. 8:14, 15); but Christ is the Son of God by birth. The writer to the Hebrews further shows that the position of the Son of God is not one to which Christ has been elevated, but that it is one which He has by right. He says that Moses was faithful in all the house of God, as a servant, "but Christ as a Son over His own house." Heb. 3:6.

And he also states that Christ is the Builder of the house. Verse 3. It is He that builds the temple of the Lord, and bears the glory. Zech. 6:12, 13.

Christ Himself taught in the most emphatic manner that He is God. When the young man came and asked, "Good Master, what shall I do that I may inherit eternal life?" Jesus, before replying to the direct question, said: "Why callest thou Me good? there is none good but One, that is, God." Mark 10:17, 18. What did Jesus mean by these words? Did He mean to disclaim the epithet as applied to Himself? Did He mean to intimate that He was not absolutely good? Was it a modest depreciation of Himself?—By no means; for Christ was absolutely good. To the Jews, who were continually watching to detect in Him some failing of which they might accuse Him, He boldly said, "Which of you convinceth Me of sin?" John 8:46. In the whole Jewish nation not a man could be found who had ever seen Him do a thing or heard Him utter a word that had even the semblance of evil; and those who were determined to condemn Him could do it only by hiring false witnesses against Him. Peter says that He "did no sin, neither was guile found in His mouth." 1 Peter 2:22. Paul says that He "knew no sin." 2 Cor. 5:21. The Psalmist says, "He is my Rock, and there is no unrighteousness in Him." Ps. 92:15. And John says, "Ye know that He was manifested to take away our sins; and in Him is no sin." 1 John 3:5.

Christ cannot deny Himself, therefore He could not say that He was not good. He is and was absolutely good, the perfection of goodness. And since there is none good but God, and Christ is good, it follows that Christ is God, and that this is what He meant to teach the young man.

It was this that He taught the disciples. When Philip said to Jesus, "Show us the Father, and it sufficeth us," Jesus said to him: "Have I been so long time with you, and yet hast thou not known Me, Philip? he that hath seen Me hath seen the Father; and how sayest thou then, Show us the Father?" John 14:8, 9. This is as emphatic as when He said, "I and My Father are one." John 10:30. So truly was Christ God, even when here among men, that when asked to exhibit the Father He could say, Behold Me. And this brings to mind the statement that when the Father brought the First-begotten into the world, He said, "And let all the angels of God worship Him." Heb. 1:6. It was not simply when Christ was sharing the glory of the Father before the world was that He was entitled to homage, but when He came a Babe in Bethlehem, even then all the angels of God were commanded to adore Him.

The Jews did not misunderstand Christ's teaching concerning Himself. When He declared that He was one with the Father, the Jews took up stones to stone Him ; and when He asked them for which of His good works they sought to stone Him, they replied: "For a good work we stone Thee not; but for blasphemy; and because that Thou, being a man, makest Thyself God." John 10:33. If He had been what they regarded Him, a mere man, His words would indeed have been blasphemy; but He was God.

The object of Christ in coming to earth was to reveal God to men, so that they might come to Him. Thus the apostle Paul says that "God was in Christ, reconciling the world unto Himself" (2 Cor. 5:19); and in John we read that the Word, which was God, was "made flesh." John 1:1, 14. In the same connection it is stated, "No man hath seen God at any time; the only-begotten Son, which is in the bosom of the Father, He hath declared Him" (or made Him known). John 1:18.

Note the expression, "the only-begotten Son, which is in the bosom of the Father." He has His abode there, and He *is* there as a part of the Godhead, as surely when on earth as when in heaven. The use of the present tense implies continued existence. It presents the same idea that is contained in the statement of Jesus to the Jews (John 8:58), "Before Abraham was, I am." And this again shows His identity with the One who appeared to Moses in the burning bush, who declared His name to be "I AM THAT I AM."

And, finally, we have the inspired words of the apostle Paul concerning Jesus Christ, that "it pleased the Father that in Him should all fullness dwell." Col. 1:19. What this fullness is, which dwells in Christ, we learn from the next chapter, where we are told that "in Him dwelleth all the fullness of the Godhead bodily." Col. 2:9. This is most absolute and unequivocal testimony to the fact that Christ possesses by nature all the attributes of Divinity. The fact of the Divinity of Christ will also appear very distinctly as we proceed to consider

CHRIST AS CREATOR.

Immediately following the oft-quoted text which says that Christ, the Word, is God, we read that "all things were made by Him; and without Him was not anything made that was made." John 1:3. Comment cannot make this statement any clearer than it is, therefore we pass to the words of Heb. 1:1–4: "God . . hath in these last days spoken unto us by His Son, whom He hath appointed heir of all things, by whom also He made the worlds; who being the brightness of His glory, and the express image of His Person, and upholding all things by the word of His power, when He had by Himself purged our sins, sat down on the right hand of the Majesty on high; being made so much better than the angels, as He hath by inheritance obtained a more excellent name than they."

Still more emphatic than this are the words of the apostle Paul to the Colossians. Speaking of Christ as the One through whom we have redemption, he describes Him as the One "who is the image of the invisible God, the first-born of every creature; for by Him were all things created, that are in heaven, and that are in earth, visible and invisible, whether they be thrones, or dominions, or principalities, or powers ; all things were created by Him, and for Him; and He is before all things, and by Him all things consist."   Col. 1:15–17.

This wonderful text should be carefully studied and often contemplated.   It leaves not a thing in the universe that Christ did not create.   He made everything in heaven, and everything on earth; He made everything that can be seen, and everything that cannot be seen; the thrones and dominions, and the principalities and the powers in heaven, all depend upon Him for existence.   And as He is before all things, and their Creator, so by Him do all things consist, or hold together.   This is equivalent to what is said in Heb. 1:3, that He upholds all things by the word of His power.   It was by a word that the heavens were made ; and that same word holds them in their place, and preserves them from destruction.

We cannot possibly omit in this connection Isa. 40: 25, 26: "To whom then will ye liken Me, or shall I be equal? saith the Holy One.   Lift up your eyes on high, and behold who hath created these things, that bringeth out their host by number ; He calleth them all by names by the greatness of His might, for that He is strong in power; not one faileth."   Or, as the Jewish translation more forcibly renders it, "from Him, who is great in might, and strong in power, not one escapeth." That Christ is the Holy One who thus calls the host of heaven by name, and holds them in their place, is evident from other portions of the same chapter. He is the One before whom it was said, "Prepare ye the way of the Lord, make straight in the desert a highway for our God." He is the One who comes with a strong hand, having His reward with Him; the One who, like a shepherd, feeds His flock, carrying the lambs in His bosom.

One more statement concerning Christ as Creator must suffice. It is the testimony of the Father Himself. In the first chapter of Hebrews, we read that God has spoken to us by His Son; that He said of Him, "Let all the angels of God worship Him;" that of the angels He saith, "Who maketh His angels spirits, and His ministers a flame of fire," but that He says to the Son, "Thy throne, O God, is forever and ever; a scepter of righteousness is the scepter of Thy kingdom;" and God says further: "Thou, Lord, in the beginning hast laid the foundation of the earth; and the heavens are the works of Thine hands." Heb. 1 : 8–10. Here we find the Father addressing the Son as God, and saying to Him, Thou hast laid the foundations of the earth; and the heavens are the work of Thy hands. When the Father Himself gives this honor to the Son, what is man, that he should withhold it? With this we may well leave the direct testimony concerning the Divinity of Christ, and the fact that He is the Creator of all things.

A word of caution may be necessary here. Let no one imagine that we would exalt Christ at the expense of the Father, or would ignore the Father. That cannot be, for their interests are one. We honor the Father in honoring the Son. We are mindful of Paul's words, that " to us there is but one God, the Father, of whom are all things, and we in Him; and one Lord Jesus Christ, by whom are all things, and we by Him " (1 Cor. 8 : 6); just as we have already quoted, that it was by Him that God made the worlds. All things proceed ultimately from God, the Father; even Christ Himself proceeded and came forth from the Father; but it has pleased the Father that in Him should all fullness dwell, and that He should be the direct, immediate Agent in every act of creation. Our object in this investigation is to set forth Christ's rightful position of equality with the Father, in order that His power to redeem may be the better appreciated.

IS CHRIST A CREATED BEING?

Before passing to some of the practical lessons that are to be learned from these truths, we must dwell for a few moments upon an opinion that is honestly held by many who would not for any consideration willingly dishonor Christ, but who, through that opinion, do actually deny His Divinity. It is the idea that Christ is a created being, who, through the good-pleasure of God, was elevated to His present lofty position. No one who holds this view can possibly have any just conception of the exalted position which Christ really occupies.

The view in question is built upon a misconception of a single text, Rev. 3 : 14: "And unto the angel of the church of the Laodiceans write : These things saith the Amen, the faithful and true Witness, the Beginning of the creation of God." This is wrongly interpreted to mean that Christ is the first being that God created; that God's work of creation began with Him. But this view antagonizes the scripture which declares that Christ Himself created all things. To say that God began His work of creation by creating Christ is to leave Christ entirely out of the work of creation.

The word rendered "beginning" is *arche*, meaning, as well, "head" or "chief." It occurs in the name of the Greek ruler, *Archon*, in *arch*bishop, and the word *arch*angel. Take this last word. Christ is the Archangel. See Jude 9; 1 Thess. 4 : 16; John 5 : 28, 29; Dan. 10 : 21. This does not mean that He is the first of the angels, for He is not an angel, but is above them. Heb. 1 : 4. It means that He is the chief or prince of the angels, just as an archbishop is the head of the bishops. Christ is the commander of the angels. See Rev. 19 : 11–14. He created the angels. Col. 1 : 16. And so the statement that He is the beginning or head of the creation of God, means that in Him creation had its beginning; that, as He Himself says, He is Alpha and Omega, the beginning and the end, the first and the last. Rev. 21:6; 22:13.· He is the source whence all things have their origin.

Neither should we imagine that Christ is a creature, because Paul calls Him (Col. 1 : 15) "the Firstborn of every creature;" for the very next verses show Him to be Creator, and not a creature. "For by Him were all things created, that are in heaven, and that are in earth, visible and invisible, whether they be thrones, or dominions, or principalities, or powers; all things were created by Him, and for Him; and He is before all things, and by Him all things consist." Now if He created everything that was ever created, and existed before all created things, it is evident that He Himself is not among created things. He is above all creation, and not a part of it.

The Scriptures declare that Christ is "the only-begotten Son of God." He is begotten, not created. As to when He was begotten, it is not for us to inquire, nor could our minds grasp it if we were told. The prophet Micah tells us all that we can know about it, in these words: "But thou, Bethlehem Ephratah, though thou be little among the thousands of Judah, yet out of thee shall He come forth unto Me that is to be ruler in Israel; whose goings forth have been from of old, from the days of eternity." Micah 5:2, margin. There was a time when Christ proceeded forth and came from God, from the bosom of the Father (John 8 : 42; 1 : 18), but that time was so far back in the days of eternity that to finite comprehension it is practically without beginning.

But the point is that Christ is a begotten Son, and not a created subject. He has *by inheritance* a more excellent Name than the angels; He is " a Son over His own house." Heb. 1 : 4; 3 : 6. And since He is the only-begotten Son of God, He is of the very substance and nature of God, and possesses by birth all the attributes of God; for the Father was pleased that His Son should be the express image of His Person, the brightness of His glory, and filled with all the fullness of the Godhead. So He has " life in Himself; " He possesses immortality in His own right, and can confer immortality upon others. Life inheres in Him, so that it cannot be taken from Him; but, having voluntarily laid it down, He can take it again. His words are these: " Therefore doth My Father love Me, because I lay down My life, that I might take it again. No man taketh it from Me, but I lay it down of Myself. I have power to lay it down, and I have power to take it again. This commandment have I received of My Father." John 10 : 17, 18.

If anyone springs the old cavil, how Christ could be immortal and yet die, we have only to say that we do not know. We make no pretensions of fathoming infinity. We cannot understand how Christ could be God in the beginning, sharing equal glory with the Father, before the world was, and still be born a babe in Bethlehem. The mystery of the crucifixion and resurrection is but the mystery of the incarnation. We cannot understand how Christ could be God and still become man for our sake. We cannot understand how He could create the world from nothing, nor how He can raise the dead, nor yet how it is that He works by His Spirit in our own hearts; yet we believe and know these things. It should be sufficient for us to accept as true those things which God has revealed, without stumbling over things that the mind of an angel cannot fathom. So we delight in the infinite power and glory which the Scriptures declare belong to Christ, without worrying our finite minds in a vain attempt to explain the infinite.

Finally, we know the Divine unity of the Father and the Son from the fact that both have the same Spirit. Paul, after saying that they that are in the flesh cannot please God, continues: "But ye are not in the flesh, but in the Spirit, if so be that the Spirit of God dwell in you. Now if any man have not the Spirit of Christ, he is none of His." Rom. 8:9. Here we find that the Holy Spirit is both the Spirit of God and the Spirit of Christ. Christ "*is* in the bosom of the Father;" being by nature of the very substance of God, and having life in Himself, He is properly called Jehovah, the self-existent One, and is thus styled in Jer. 23:56, where it is said that the righteous Branch, who shall execute judgment and justice in the earth, shall be known by the name of *Jehovah-tsidckcnu*— THE LORD, OUR RIGHTEOUSNESS.

Let no one, therefore, who honors Christ at all, give Him less honor than he gives the Father, for this would be to dishonor the Father by just so much; but let all, with the angels in heaven, worship the Son, having no fear that they are worshiping and serving the creature instead of the Creator.

And now, while the matter of Christ's Divinity is fresh in our minds, let us pause to consider the wonderful story of His humiliation.

GOD MANIFEST IN THE FLESH.

"And the Word was made flesh, and dwelt among us." John 1:14.

No words could more plainly show that Christ was both God and man. Originally only Divine, He took upon Himself human nature, and passed among men as only a common mortal, except at those times when his Divinity flashed through, as on the occasion of the cleansing of the temple, or when His burning words of simple truth forced even His enemies to confess that "never man spake like this man."

The humiliation which Christ voluntarily took upon Himself is best expressed by Paul to the Philippians: "Have this mind in you which was also in Christ Jesus; who being originally in the form of

God, counted it not a thing to be grasped [that is, to be clung to] to be on an equality with God, but emptied Himself, taking the form of a bond-servant, becoming in the likeness of men; and being found in fashion as a man, He humbled Himself, becoming obedient even unto death, yea, the death of the cross." Phil. 2:5–8, Revised Version, marginal reading.

The above rendering makes this text much more plain than it is in the common version. The idea is that, although Christ was in the form of God, being " the brightness of His glory, and the express image of His Person" (Heb. 1:3), having all the attributes of God, being the Ruler of the universe, and the One whom all Heaven delighted to honor, He did not think that any of these things were to be desired, so long as men were lost and without strength. He could not enjoy His glory while man was an outcast, without hope. So He emptied Himself, divested Himself of all His riches and His glory, and took upon Himself the nature of man, in order that He might redeem him. And so we may reconcile Christ's unity with the Father with the statement, "My Father is greater than I."

It is impossible for us to understand how Christ could, as God, humble Himself to the death of the cross, and it is worse than useless for us to speculate about it. All we can do is to accept the facts as they are presented in the Bible. If the reader finds it difficult to harmonize some of the statements in the Bible concerning the nature of Christ, let him remember that it would be impossible to express it in terms that would enable finite minds to grasp it fully. Just as the grafting of the Gentiles into the stock of Israel is contrary to nature, so much of the Divine economy is a paradox to human understanding.

Other scriptures that we will quote bring closer to us the fact of the humanity of Christ, and what it means for us. We have already read that "the Word was made flesh," and now we will read what Paul says concerning the nature of that flesh: "For what the law could not do, in that it was weak through the flesh, God sending his own Son in the likeness of sinful flesh, and for sin, condemned sin in the flesh; that the righteousness of the law might be fulfilled in us, who walk not after the flesh, but after the Spirit." Rom. 8:3, 4.

A little thought will be sufficient to show anybody that if Christ took upon Himself the likeness of man, in order that He might redeem man, it must have been sinful man that He was made like, for it is sinful man that He came to redeem. Death could have no power over a sinless man, as Adam was in Eden; and it could not have had any power over Christ, if the Lord had not laid on Him the iniquity of us all. Moreover, the fact that Christ took upon Himself the flesh, not of a sinless being, but of sinful man, that is, that the flesh which He assumed had all the weaknesses and sinful tendencies to which fallen human nature is subject, is shown by the statement that He " was made of the seed of David *according to the flesh.*" David had all the passions of human nature. He says of himself, " Behold, I was shapen in iniquity; and in sin did my mother conceive me." Ps. 51 : 5.

The following statement in the book of Hebrews is very clear on this point:—

"For verily He took not on Him the nature of angels; but He took on Him the seed of Abraham. ["For verily not of angels doth He take hold, but He taketh hold of the seed of Abraham." Revised Version.] Wherefore in all things it behooved Him to be made like unto His brethren, that He might be a merciful and faithful high priest in things pertaining to God, to make reconciliation for the sins of the people. For in that He Himself hath suffered being tempted, He is able to succor them that are tempted." Heb. 2:16-18.

If He was made in all things like unto His brethren, then He must have suffered all the infirmities, and been subject to all the temptations, of His brethren. Two more texts that put this matter very forcibly will be sufficient evidence on this point. We first quote 2 Cor. 5:21:—

"For He [God] hath made Him [Christ] to be sin for us, who knew no sin; that we might be made the righteousness of God in Him."

This is much stronger than the statement that He was made "in the likeness of sinful flesh." He was *made to be sin.* Here is the same mystery as that the Son of God should die. The spotless Lamb of God, who knew no sin, was made to be sin. Sinless, yet not only counted as a sinner, but

actually taking upon Himself sinful nature.   *He*
was made to be sin in order that *we* might be made
righteousness.   So Paul says to the Galatians that
" God sent forth His Son, made of a woman, made
under the law, to redeem them that were under the
law, that we might receive the adoption of sons."
Gal. 4:4, 5.

"In that He Himself hath suffered being tempted, He is
able to succor them that are tempted."   "For we have not
a High Priest which cannot be touched with the feeling of
our infirmities; but was in all points tempted like as we are,
yet without sin.   Let us therefore come boldly unto the
throne of grace, that we may obtain mercy, and find grace
to help in time of need."   Heb. 2:18; 4:15, 16.

One more point, and then we can learn the entire
lesson that we should learn from the fact that "the
Word was made flesh, and dwelt among us."   How
was it that Christ could be thus "compassed with
infirmity" (Heb. 5:2), and still know no sin?   Some
may have thought, while reading thus far, that we
were depreciating the character of Jesus, by bringing him down to the level of sinful man.   On the
contrary, we are simply exalting the "Divine power"
of our blessed Saviour, who Himself voluntarily descended to the level of sinful man, in order that He
might exalt man to His own spotless purity, which
He retained under the most adverse circumstances.
His humanity only veiled His Divine nature, by
which He was inseparably connected with the invisible God, and which was more than able success-
fully to resist the weaknesses of the flesh.   There

was in His whole life a struggle. The flesh, moved upon by the enemy of all righteousness, would tend to sin, yet His Divine nature never for a moment harbored an evil desire, nor did His Divine power for a moment waver. Having suffered in the flesh all that men can possibly suffer, He returned to the throne of the Father as spotless as when He left the courts of glory. When He lay in the tomb, under the power of death, "it was impossible that He should be holden of it," because He "knew no sin."

But someone will say, "I don't see any comfort in this for me. To be sure, I have an example, but I can't follow it, for I haven't the power that Christ had. He was God even while here on earth; I am but a man." Yes, but you may have the same power that He had if you want it. He was "compassed with infirmity," yet He "did no sin," because of the Divine power constantly dwelling within Him. Now listen to the inspired words of the apostle Paul, and learn what it is our privilege to have:—

"For this cause I bow my knees unto the Father of our Lord Jesus Christ, of whom the whole family in heaven and earth is named, that He would grant you, according to the riches of His glory, to be strengthened with might by His Spirit in the inner man; that *Christ may dwell in your hearts* by faith; that ye, being rooted and grounded in love, may be able to comprehend with all saints what is the breadth, and length, and depth, and height; and to know the love of Christ, which passeth knowledge, that *ye might be filled with all the fullness of God.*" Eph. 3:14-19.

Who could ask for more? Christ, in whom

dwelleth all the fullness of the Godhead bodily, may dwell in our hearts, so that we may be filled with all the fullness of God.   What a wonderful promise! He is "touched with the feeling of our infirmity." That is, having suffered all that sinful flesh is heir to, He knows all about it, and so closely does He identify Himself with His children that whatever presses upon them makes a like impression upon Him, and He knows how much Divine power is necessary to resist it; and if we but sincerely desire to deny "ungodliness and worldly lusts," He is able and anxious to give to us strength "exceeding abundantly, above all that we ask or think."   All the power which Christ had dwelling in Him by nature, we may have dwelling in us by grace, for He freely bestows it upon us.

Then let the weary, feeble, sin-oppressed souls take courage.   Let them "come boldly unto the throne of grace," where they are sure to find grace to help in time of need, because that need is felt by our Saviour in the very time of need.   He is "touched with the feeling of our infirmity."   If it were simply that He suffered eighteen hundred years ago, we might fear that He had forgotten some of the infirmity; but no, the very temptation that presses you touches Him.   His wounds are ever fresh, and He ever lives to make intercession for you.

What wonderful possibilities there are for the Christian!   To what heights of holiness he may attain! No matter how much Satan may war against him, assaulting him where the flesh is weakest, he may abide under the shadow of the Almighty, and be filled with the fullness of God's strength.   The One stronger than Satan may dwell in his heart continually; and so, looking at Satan's assaults as from a strong fortress, he may say, "I can do all things through Christ, which strengtheneth me."

IMPORTANT PRACTICAL LESSONS.

It is not merely as a beautiful theory, a mere dogma, that we should consider Christ as God and Creator. Every doctrine of the Bible is for our practical benefit, and should be studied for that purpose. Let us first see what relation this doctrine sustains to the central commandment of the law of God. In Gen. 2:1–3 we find these words closing the record of creation: "Thus the heavens and the earth were finished, and all the host of them. And on the seventh day God ended His work which He had made; and He rested on the seventh day from all His work which He had made.   And God blessed the seventh day, and sanctified it; because that in it He had rested from all His work which God created and made."   The Jewish translation renders the text more literally thus: "Thus were finished the heavens and the earth, and all their host.   And God had finished on the seventh day His work which He had made," etc.   This is the same that we find in the fourth commandment, Ex. 20:8–11.

In this we find, what is most natural, that the same Being who created, rested. He who worked six days in creating the earth, rested on the seventh, and blessed and sanctified it. But we have already learned that God the Father created the worlds by His Son Jesus Christ, and that Christ created everything that has an existence. Therefore the conclusion is inevitable that Christ rested on that first seventh day, at the close of the six days of creation, and that He blessed and sanctified it. Thus the seventh day—the Sabbath—is most emphatically the Lord's day. When Jesus said to the carping Pharisees, "For the Son of man is Lord even of the Sabbath-day" (Matt. 12:8), He declared his lordship of the identical day which they so scrupulously observed in form; and He did this in words which show that He regarded it as His badge of authority, as demonstrating the fact that He was greater than the temple. Thus, the seventh day is the Divinely-appointed memorial of creation. It is the most honored of all days, since its especial mission is to bring to mind the creative power of God, which is the one proof to man of His Divinity. And so when Christ said that the Son of Man is Lord *even of the Sabbath-day*, He claimed a high distinction—nothing less than being the Creator, of whose Divinity that day stands as a memorial.

What shall we say, then, to the suggestion often made, that Christ changed the day of the Sabbath from a day which commemorates completed crea-

tion to one which has no such significance?
Simply this, that for Christ to change or abolish
the Sabbath would be to destroy that which calls to
mind His Divinity. If Christ had abolished the Sabbath, He would have undone the work of His own
hands, and thus have worked against Himself; and
a kingdom divided against itself cannot stand.
But Christ "cannot deny Himself," and therefore
He did not change one jot of that which He Himself appointed, and which, by testifying to His Divinity, shows Him to be worthy of honor above all
the gods of the heathen. It would have been as
impossible for Christ to change the Sabbath as it
would have been to change the fact that He created
all things in six days, and rested on the seventh.

Again, the oft-repeated declarations that the Lord
is Creator are intended as a source of strength.
Notice how creation and redemption are connected
in the first chapter of Colossians.   To get the point
fully before us, we will read verses 9–19:—

"For this cause we also, since the day we heard it, do not
cease to pray for you, and to desire that ye might be filled
with the knowledge of His will in all wisdom and spiritual
understanding; that ye might walk worthy of the Lord unto
all pleasing, being fruitful in every good work, and increasing in the knowledge of God; strengthened with all might,
according to His glorious power, unto all patience and long-
suffering with joyfulness; giving thanks unto the Father,
which hath made us meet to be partakers of the inheritance
of the saints in light; who hath delivered us from the power
of darkness, and hath translated us into the kingdom of His
dear Son; in whom we have redemption through His blood,

even the forgiveness of sins; who is the image of the invisible God, the First-born of every creature; for by Him were all things created, that are in heaven, and that are in earth, visible and invisible, whether they be thrones, or dominions, or principalities, or powers; all things were created by Him, and for Him; and He is before all things, and in Him all things consist. And He is the Head of the body, the Church; who is the Beginning, the First-born from the dead; that in all things He might have the pre-eminence. For it pleased the Father that in Him should all fullness dwell."

It is not an accident that the wonderful declaration concerning Christ as Creator is connected with the statement that in Him we have redemption. No; when the apostle makes known his desire that we should be "strengthened with all might, according to His glorious power," he lets us know what that glorious power is. When he tells us about being delivered from the power of darkness, he lets us know something of the power of the Deliverer. It is for our comfort that we are told that the head of the church is the Creator of all things. We are told that He upholds all things by the word of His power (Heb. 1:3), in order that we may rest in the assurance that

"The Hand which bears all nature up
Shall guard His children well."

Note the connection of Isa. 40: 26. The chapter presents the wonderful wisdom and power of Christ, in calling all the host of heaven by names, and in keeping them all in their places, by the greatness of His might and the strength of His power, and then inquires: "Why sayest thou, O Jacob, and speakest, O Israel, My way is hid from the Lord, and my judgment is passed over from my God? Hast thou not known? hast thou not heard, that the everlasting God, the Lord, the Creator of the ends of the earth, fainteth not, neither is weary? there is no searching of His understanding." On the contrary, "He giveth power to the faint; and to them that have no might He increaseth strength." His power is, in fact, the ability to create everything from nothing; therefore He can work wonders through those who have no strength. He can bring strength out of weakness. Surely, then, anything which serves to keep before the mind the creative power of Christ, must tend to renew our spiritual strength and courage.

And this is just the design of the Sabbath. Read the ninety-second psalm, which is entitled a psalm for the Sabbath-day. The first four verses are these:

"It is a good thing to give thanks unto the Lord, and to sing praises unto Thy name, O Most High; to show forth Thy loving-kindness in the morning, and Thy faithfulness every night, upon an instrument of ten strings, and upon the psaltery; upon the harp with a solemn sound. For Thou, Lord, hast made me glad through Thy work; I will triumph in the works of Thy hands.'

What has this to do with the Sabbath? Just this: The Sabbath is the memorial of creation. Says the Lord: "Moreover also I gave them My sabbaths, to be a sign between Me and them, that they might know that I am the Lord that sanctify them." Eze. 20 : 12. The Psalmist kept the Sabbath as God designed that it should be kept—in meditating upon creation and the wondrous power and goodness of God displayed therein. And then, thinking of that, he realized that the God who clothes the lilies with a glory surpassing that of Solomon, cares far more for His intelligent creatures; and as he looked at the heavens, which show the power and glory of God, and realized that they were brought into existence from nothing, the encouraging thought would come to him that this same power would work in him to deliver him from human infirmity. Therefore he was glad, and he triumphed in the work of God's hands. The knowledge of God's power, which came to him through a contemplation of creation, filled him with courage, as he realized that the same power was at his disposal; and, grasping that power by faith, he gained victories through it. And this is the design of the Sabbath; it is to bring man to a saving knowledge of God.

The argument, concisely stated, is this: 1. Faith in God is begotten by a knowledge of His power; to distrust Him implies ignorance of His ability to perform His promises; our faith in Him must be in proportion to our real knowledge of His power. 2. An intelligent contemplation of God's creation gives us a true conception of His power; for His eternal power and Godhead are understood by the things which He has made. Rom. 1 : 20. 3. It is faith that gives victory (1 John 5 : 4); therefore, since faith comes by learning the power of God, from His word and from the things that He has made, we gain the victory, or triumph through the works of His hands. The Sabbath, therefore, which is the memorial of creation, is, if properly observed, a source of the Christian's greatest re-inforcement in battle.

This is the import of Eze. 20 : 12: " Moreover, also, I gave them My Sabbaths, to be a sign between Me and them, that they might know that I am the Lord that sanctify them." That is, knowing that our sanctification is the will of God (1 Thess. 4 : 3; 5 : 23, 24), we learn, by means of the Sabbath, properly used, what the power of God is that is exerted for our sanctification. The same power that was put forth to create the worlds is put forth for the sanctification of those who yield themselves to the will of God. Surely this thought, when fully grasped, must bring joy and comfort in God to the earnest soul. In the light of this, we can appreciate the force of Isa. 58 : 13, 14:—

" If thou turn away thy foot from the Sabbath, from doing thy pleasure on My holy day; and call the Sabbath a delight, the holy of the Lord, honorable; and shalt honor Him, not doing thine own ways, nor finding thine own pleasure, nor speaking thine own words; *then shalt thou delight thyself in the Lord;* and I will cause thee to ride upon the high places of the earth, and feed thee with the heritage of Jacob thy father; for the mouth of the Lord hath spoken it."

That is, if the Sabbath is kept according to God's

plan, as a memorial of His creative power, as bringing to mind the Divine power that is put forth for the salvation of His people, the soul, triumphing in the work of His hands, must delight itself in the Lord. And so the Sabbath is the grand fulcrum for the lever of faith, which lifts the soul to the heights of God's throne, to hold communion with Him.

To put the matter in few words, it may be stated thus: The eternal power and Godhead of the Lord are revealed in creation. Rom. 1 : 20. It is the ability to create that measures the power of God. But the Gospel is the power of God unto salvation. Rom. 1 : 16. Therefore the Gospel simply reveals to us the power which was used to bring the worlds into existence, now exerted for the salvation of men. It is the same power in each case.

In the light of this great truth, there is no room for the controversy about redemption being greater than creation, because redemption *is* creation. See 2 Cor. 5 : 17; Eph. 4 : 24. The power of redemption is the power of creation; the power of God unto salvation is the power which can take human nothingness and make of it that which shall be throughout eternal ages to the praise of the glory of the grace of God. "Wherefore let them that suffer according to the will of God commit the keeping of their souls to Him in well doing, as unto a faithful Creator." 1 Peter 4 : 19.

CHRIST THE LAWGIVER.

"For the Lord is our Judge, the Lord is our Lawgiver, the Lord is our King; He will save us." Isa. 33: 22.

We have now to consider Christ in another character, yet not another. It is one that naturally results from His position as Creator, for the One who creates must certainly have authority to guide and control. We read in John 5 : 22, 23 the words of Christ, that "the Father judgeth no man, but hath committed all judgment unto the Son; that all men should honor the Son even as they honor the Father." As Christ is the manifestation of the Father in creation, so is He the manifestation of the Father in giving and executing the law. A few texts of Scripture will suffice to prove this.

In Num. 21 : 4–6 we have the partial record of an incident that took place while the children of Israel were in the wilderness. Let us read it: "And they journeyed from Mount Hor by the way of the Red Sea, to compass the land of Edom; and the soul of the people was much discouraged because of the way. And the people spake against God, and against Moses, Wherefore have ye brought us up out of Egypt to die in the wilderness? for there is no bread, neither is there any water; and our soul loatheth this light bread. And the Lord sent fiery serpents among the people, and they bit the people; and much people of Israel died." The people spoke against God and against Moses, saying,

Why have ye brought us up into the wilderness?
They found fault with their Leader. This is why
they were destroyed by serpents. Now read the
words of the apostle Paul concerning this same
event:—

"Neither let us tempt Christ, as some of them
also tempted, and were destroyed of serpents." 1
Cor. 10:9. What does this prove?—That the Leader
against whom they were murmuring was Christ.
This is further proved by the fact that when Moses
cast in his lot with Israel, refusing to be called the
son of Pharaoh's daughter, he esteemed the reproach
of Christ greater riches than the treasures of Egypt.
Heb. 11:26. Read also 1 Cor. 10:4, where Paul
says that the fathers "did all drink the same spiritual drink; for they drank of that spiritual Rock that
followed them; and that Rock was Christ." So,
then, Christ was the Leader of Israel from Egypt.

The third chapter of Hebrews makes clear this
same fact. Here we are told to consider the
Apostle and High Priest of our profession, Christ
Jesus, who was faithful in all His house, not
as a servant, but as a Son over His own house.
Verses 1–6. Then we are told that we are His
house if we hold fast our confidence to the end.
Wherefore we are exhorted by the Holy Ghost to
hear His voice and not to harden our hearts, as the
fathers did in the wilderness. "For we are made
partakers of Christ, if we hold the beginning of our
confidence steadfast unto the end; while it is said,

To-day if ye will hear His [Christ's] voice, harden not your hearts, as in the provocation. For some, when they had heard, did provoke; howbeit not all that came out of Egypt by Moses. But with whom was He [Christ] grieved forty years? was it not with them that had sinned, whose carcasses fell in the wilderness?" Verses 14–17. Here again Christ is set forth as the leader and commander of Israel in their forty years' sojourn in the wilderness.

The same thing is shown in Josh. 5 : 13–15, where we are told that the man whom Joshua saw by Jericho, having a sword drawn in his hand, in response to Joshua's question, "Art thou for us, or for our adversaries?" said, " Nay; but as Captain of the host of the Lord am I now come." Indeed, no one will be found to dispute that Christ was the real Leader of Israel, although invisible. Moses, the visible leader of Israel, " endured as seeing Him who is invisible." It was Christ who commissioned Moses to go and deliver His people. Now read Ex. 20 : 1–3 :—

"And God spake all these words, saying, I am the Lord thy God, which have brought thee out of the land of Egypt, out of the house of bondage. Thou shalt have no other gods before Me." Who spoke these words?—The One who brought them from Egypt. And who was the Leader of Israel from Egypt?—It was Christ. Then who spoke the law from Mt. Sinai?—It was Christ, the brightness of the Father's glory, and the express image of His

Person, who is the manifestation of God to man. It was the Creator of all created things, and the One to whom all judgment has been committed.

This point may be proved in another way. When the Lord comes, it will be with a shout (1 Thess. 4:16), which will pierce the tombs and arouse the dead (John 5:28, 29). "The Lord shall roar from on high, and utter His voice from His holy habitation; He shall mightily roar upon His habitation; He shall give a shout, as they that tread the grapes, against all the inhabitants of the earth. A noise shall come even to the ends of the earth; for the Lord hath a controversy with the nations, He will plead with all flesh; He will give them that are wicked to the sword, saith the Lord." Jer. 25:30, 31. Comparing this with Rev. 19:11–21, where Christ as the Leader of the armies of heaven, the Word of God, King of kings, and Lord of lords, goes forth to tread the wine-press of the fierceness and wrath of Almighty God, destroying all the wicked, we find that it is Christ who roars from His habitation against all the inhabitants of the earth, when He has His controversy with the nations. Joel adds another point, when he says, "The Lord also shall roar out of Zion, and utter His voice from Jerusalem; and the heavens and the earth shall shake." Joel 3:16.

From these texts, to which others might be added, we learn that, in connection with the coming of the Lord to deliver His people, he speaks with a voice that shakes the earth and the heavens,—"the earth shall reel to and fro like a drunkard, and shall be removed like a cottage" (Isa. 24: 20), and "the heavens shall pass away with a great noise" (2 Peter 3: 10). Now read Heb. 12: 25, 26:—

"See that ye refuse not Him that speaketh; for if they es caped not who refused Him that spake on earth, much more shall not we escape, if we turn away from Him that speaketh from heaven; whose voice then shook the earth; but now He hath promised, saying, Yet once more I shake not the earth only, but also heaven."

The time when the Voice speaking on earth shook the earth was when the law was spoken from Sinai (Ex. 19: 18–20; Heb. 12: 18–20), an event that for awfulness has never had a parallel, and never will have until the Lord comes with all the angels of heaven, to save His people. But note: The same voice that then shook the earth will, in the coming time, shake not only earth, but heaven also; and we have seen that it is the voice of Christ that will sound with such volume as to shake heaven and earth when He has His controversy with the nations. Therefore it is demonstrated that it was the voice of Christ that was heard from Sinai, proclaiming the ten commandments. This is no more than would naturally be concluded from what we have learned concerning Christ as Creator, and the Maker of the Sabbath.

Indeed, the fact that Christ is a part of the Godhead, possessing all the attributes of Divinity, being the equal of the Father in all respects, as Creator and Lawgiver, is the only force there is in the atonement. It is this alone which makes redemption a possibility. Christ died "that He might bring us to God" (1 Peter 3 : 18); but if He lacked one iota of being equal to God, He could not bring us to Him. Divinity means having the attributes of Deity. If Christ were not Divine, then we should have only a human sacrifice. It matters not, even if it be granted that Christ was the highest created intelligence in the universe; in that case He would be a subject, owing allegiance to the law, without ability to do any more than His own duty. He could have no righteousness to impart to others. There is an infinite distance between the highest angel ever created, and God; therefore the highest angel could not lift fallen man up, and make him partaker of the Divine nature. Angels can minister; God only can redeem. Thanks be to God that we are saved "through the redemption that is in Christ Jesus," in whom dwelleth all the fullness of the Godhead bodily, and who is, therefore, able to save to the uttermost them that come unto God by Him.

This truth helps to a more perfect understanding of the reason why Christ is called the Word of God. He is the One through whom the Divine will and the Divine power are made known to men. He is, so to speak, the mouth-piece of Divinity, the manifestation of the Godhead. He declares or makes God known to man. It pleased the Father that in Him should all fullness dwell; and therefore the Father is not relegated to a secondary position, as some imagine, when Christ is exalted as Creator and Lawgiver; for the glory of the Father shines through the Son. Since God is known only through Christ, it is evident that the Father cannot be honored as He ought to be honored, by those who do not exalt Christ. As Christ Himself said, " He that honoreth not the Son honoreth not the Father which hath sent Him." John 5 : 23.

Is·it asked how Christ could be the Mediator between God and man and also the Lawgiver? We have not to explain how it can be but only to accept the Scripture record that it is so. And the fact that it is so is that which gives strength to the doctrine of the atonement. The sinner's surety of full and free pardon lies in the fact that the Lawgiver Himself, the One against whom he has rebelled and whom he has defied, is the One who gave Himself for us. How is it possible for anyone to doubt the honesty of God's purpose, or His perfect good-will to men, when He gave Himself for their redemption? for let it not be imagined that the Father and the Son were separated in this transaction. They were one in this, as in everything else. The counsel of peace was between them both (Zech. 6: 12, 13), and even while here on earth the only-begotten Son was in the bosom of the Father.

What a wonderful manifestation of love! The Innocent suffered for the guilty; the Just, for the unjust; the Creator, for the creature; the Maker of the law, for the transgressor against the law; the King, for his rebellious subjects. Since God spared not His own Son, but freely delivered Him up for us all;—since Christ voluntarily gave Himself for us;—how shall He not with Him freely give us all things? Infinite Love could find no greater manifestation of itself. Well may the Lord say, " What could have been done more to My vineyard, that I have not done in it?"

THE RIGHTEOUSNESS OF GOD.

" But seek ye first the kingdom of God, and His righteousness; and all these things shall be added unto you." Matt. 6:33.

The righteousness of God, says Jesus, is the one thing to be sought in this life. Food and clothing are minor matters in comparison with it. God will supply them, as a matter of course, so that anxious care and worriment need not be expended on them; but to secure God's kingdom and His righteousness should be the only object of life.

In 1 Cor. 1:30 we are told that Christ is made unto us righteousness as well as wisdom; and since Christ is the wisdom of God, and in Him dwelleth all the fullness of the Godhead bodily, it is evident that the righteousness which He is made to us is the righteousness of God. Let us see what this righteousness is.

In Ps. 119:172 the Psalmist thus addresses the Lord: "My tongue shall speak of Thy word; for all Thy commandments are righteousness." The commandments are righteousness, not simply in the abstract, but they are the righteousness of God. For proof read the following:—

"Lift up your eyes to the heavens, and look upon the earth beneath; for the heavens shall vanish away like smoke, and the earth shall wax old like a garment, and they that dwell therein shall die in like manner; but My salvation shall be forever, and My righteousness shall not be abolished. Hearken unto Me, ye that know righteousness, the people in whose heart is My law; fear ye not the reproach of men, neither be ye afraid of their revilings." Isa. 51:6, 7.

What do we learn from this?—That they who know the righteousness of God are those in whose heart is His law, and therefore that the law of God is the righteousness of God.

This may be proved again, as follows: "All unrighteousness is sin." 1 John 5:17. "Whosoever committeth sin transgresseth also the law; for sin is the transgression of the law." 1 John 3:4. Sin is the transgression of the law, and it is also unrighteousness; therefore sin and unrighteousness are identical. But if *un*righteousness is transgression of the law, righteousness must be obedience to the law. Or, to put the proposition into mathematical form:—

Unrighteousness=sin. 1 John 5:17.
Transgression of the law=sin. 1 John 3:4.

Therefore, according to the axiom that two things that are equal to the same thing are equal to each other, we have:—

Unrighteousness=transgression of the law

which is a negative equation. The same thing, stated in positive terms, would be:—

Righteousness=obedience to the law.

Now what law is it obedience to which is righteousness and disobedience to which is sin? It is that law which says, "Thou shalt not covet;" for the apostle Paul tells us that this law convinced him of sin. Rom. 7:7. The law of ten commandments, then, is the measure of the righteousness of God. Since it is the law of God, and is righteousness, it must be the righteousness of God. There is, indeed, no other righteousness.

Since the law is the righteousness of God—a transcript of His character—it is easy to see that to fear God and keep His commandments is the whole duty of man. Eccl. 12:13. Let no one think that his duty will be circumscribed if confined to the ten commandments, for they are "exceeding broad." "The law is spiritual," and comprehends a great deal more than can be discerned by an ordinary reader. "The natural man receiveth not the things of the Spirit of God; for they are foolishness unto him; neither can he know them, because they are spiritually discerned." 1 Cor. 2:14. The exceeding breadth of the law of God can be realized only by those who have prayerfully meditated upon it. A few texts of Scripture will suffice to show us something of its breadth.

In the sermon on the mount Christ said: "Ye have heard that it was said by them of old time,

Thou shalt not kill; and whosoever shall kill shall be in danger of the judgment; but I say unto you, That whosoever is angry with his brother without a cause shall be in danger of the judgment; and whosoever shall say to his brother, Raca, shall be in danger of the council; but whosoever shall say, Thou fool, shall be in danger of hell fire." Matt. 5:21,22. And again: "Ye have heard that it was said by them of old time, Thou shalt not commit adultery; but I say unto you, That whosoever looketh on a woman to lust after her hath committed adultery with her already in his heart." Verses 27, 28.

This does not mean that the commandments, "Thou shalt not kill," and, "Thou shalt not commit adultery," are imperfect, or that God now requires a greater degree of morality from Christians than He did from His people who were called Jews. He requires the same from all men in all ages. The Saviour simply explained these commandments, and showed their spirituality. To the unspoken charge of the Pharisees, that He was ignoring and undermining the moral law, He replied by saying that He came for the purpose of establishing the law, and that it could not be abolished; and then He expounded the true meaning of the law in a way that convicted them of ignoring and disobeying it. He showed that even a look or a thought may be a violation of the law, and that it is indeed a discerner of the thoughts and intents of the heart

In this Christ did not reveal a new truth, but only brought to light and unfolded an old one. The law meant just as much when He proclaimed it from Sinai as when He expounded it on the mountain in Judea. When, in tones that shook the earth, He said, "Thou shalt not kill," He meant, "Thou shalt not cherish anger in the heart; thou shalt not indulge in envy, nor strife, nor anything which is in the remotest degree akin to murder." All this and much more is contained in the words, "Thou shalt not kill." And this was taught by the inspired words of the Old Testament; for Solomon showed that the law deals with things unseen as well as things seen, when he wrote:—

"Let us hear the conclusion of the whole matter: Fear God, and keep His commandments; for this is the whole duty of man. For God shall bring every work into judgment, with every secret thing, whether it be good, or whether it be evil." Eccl. 12: 13, 14.

The argument is this: The judgment passes upon every secret thing; the law of God is the standard in the judgment,—it determines the quality of every act, whether good or evil; therefore the law of God forbids evil in thought as well as in deed. So the conclusion of the whole matter is that the commandments of God contain the whole duty of man.

Take the first commandment, "Thou shalt have no other gods before Me." The apostle tells us of some "whose god is their belly." Phil. 3 : 19. But gluttony and intemperance are self-murder; and so

we find that the first commandment runs through
to the sixth.   This is not all, however, for he also
tells us that covetousness is idolatry.   Col. 3 : 5.
The tenth commandment cannot be violated without violating the first and the second.   In other
words, the tenth commandment coincides with the
first; and we find that the decalogue is a circle having a circumference as great as the universe, and
containing within it the moral duty of every creature.   In short, it is the measure of the righteousness of God, who inhabits eternity.

This being the case, the correctness of the statement that "the doers of the law shall be justified,"
is obvious.   To *justify* means to *make righteous*, or
to show one to be righteous.   Now it is evident
that perfect obedience to a perfectly righteous law
would constitute one a righteous person.   It was
God's design that such obedience should be rendered to the law by all His creatures; and in this
way the law was ordained unto life.   Rom. 7 : 10.

But for one to be judged "a doer of the law" it
would be necessary that he had kept the law in its
fullest measure every moment of his life.   If he
had come short of this, he could not be said to
have done the law.   He could not be a doer of the
law if he had done it only in part.   It is a sad fact,
therefore, that there are in all the human race no
doers of the law, for both Jews and Gentiles are
"all under sin; as it is written, There is none righteous, no, not one; there is none that understand-

eth, there is none that seeketh after God. They are all gone out of the way, they are together become unprofitable; there is none that doeth good, no, not one." Rom. 3:9–12. The law speaks to all who are within its sphere; and in all the world there is not one who can open his mouth to clear himself from the charge of sin which it brings against him. Every mouth is stopped, and all the world stands guilty before God (verse 19), "For all have sinned, and come short of the glory of God" (verse 23).

Therefore, although "the doers of the law shall be justified," it is just as evident that "by the deeds of the law there shall no flesh be justified in His sight; for by the law is the knowledge of sin." Verse 20. The law, being "holy, and just, and good," cannot justify a sinner. In other words, a just law cannot declare that the one who violates it is innocent. A law that would justify a wicked man would be a wicked law. The law should not be reviled because it cannot justify sinners. On the contrary, it should be extolled on that account. The fact that the law will not declare sinners to be righteous,—that it will not say that men have kept it when they have violated it,—is in itself sufficient evidence that it is good. Men applaud an incorruptible earthly judge, one who cannot be bribed, and who will not declare a guilty man innocent. Surely, they ought to magnify the law of God, which will not bear false witness. It is the perfec-

tion of righteousness, and therefore it is forced to
declare the sad fact that not one of Adam's race
has fulfilled its requirements.

Moreover, the fact that to do the law is simply
man's duty shows that when he has come short in
a single particular he can never make it up. The
requirements of each precept of the law are so
broad,—the whole law is so spiritual,—that an angel could render no more than simple obedience.
Yea, more, the law is the righteousness of God,—
a transcript of His character,—and since His character cannot be different from what it is, it follows
that even God Himself cannot be better than the
measure of goodness demanded by His law. He
cannot be better than He is, and the law declares
what He is. What hope, then, that one who has
failed, in even one precept, can add enough extra
goodness to make up the full measure? He who
attempts to do that sets before himself the impossible task of being better than God requires, yea,
even better than God Himself.

But it is not simply in one particular that men
have failed. They have come short in every particular. "They are all gone out of the way, they
are together become unprofitable; there is none that
doeth good, no, not one." Not only so, but it is
impossible for fallen man, with his weakened power,
to do even a single act that is up to the perfect
standard. This proposition needs no further proof
than a restatement of the fact that the law is the

measure of God's righteousness.   Surely there are
none so presumptuous as to claim that any act of
their lives has been or could be as good as if done
by the Lord Himself.   Everyone must say with the
Psalmist, "My goodness extendeth not to Thee."
Ps. 16: 2.

This fact is contained in direct statements of
Scripture.   Christ, who "needed not that any
should testify of man; for He knew what was in
man" (John 2: 25), said: "For from within, out of
the heart of men, proceed evil thoughts, adulteries,
fornication, murders, thefts, covetousness, wicked-
ness, deceit, lasciviousness, an evil eye, blasphemy,
pride, foolishness; all these evil things come from
within, and defile the man."   Mark 7: 21–23.   In
other words, it is easier to do wrong than it is to
do right, and the things which a person naturally
does are evil.   Evil dwells within, and is a part of
the being.   Therefore the apostle says: "The carnal [fleshly, natural] mind is enmity against God;
for it is not subject to the law of God, neither indeed can be.   So then they that are in the flesh
cannot please God."   Rom. 8: 7, 8.   And again:
"The flesh lusteth against the Spirit, and the Spirit
against the flesh; and these are contrary the one to
the other; so that ye cannot do the things that ye
would."   Gal. 5: 17.   Since evil is a part of man's
very nature, being inherited by each individual
from a long line of sinful ancestors, it is very evident that whatever righteousness springs from him

must be only like "filthy rags" (Isa. 64: 6), com-
pared with the spotless robe of the righteousness
of God.

The impossibility of good deeds proceeding from
a sinful heart is thus forcibly illustrated by the Saviour: "For every tree is known by his own fruit.
For of thorns men do not gather figs, nor of a
bramble-bush gather they grapes. A good man
out of the good treasure of his heart bringeth forth
that which is good; and an evil man out of the evil
treasure of his heart bringeth forth that which is
evil; for of the abundance of the heart his mouth
speaketh." Luke 6: 44, 45. That is to say, a man
cannot do good until he first becomes good. Therefore, deeds done by a sinful person have no effect
whatever to make him righteous, but, on the contrary, coming from an evil heart, they are evil, and
so add to the sum of his sinfulness. Only evil can
come from an evil heart, and multiplied evil cannot
make one good deed; therefore it is useless for an
evil person to think to become righteous by his own
efforts. He must first be made righteous before he
can do the good that is required of him, and which
he wants to do.

The case, then, stands thus: 1. The law of God
is perfect righteousness; and perfect conformity to
it is demanded of everyone who shall enter the
kingdom of heaven. 2. But the law has not a par-
ticle of righteousness to bestow upon any man, for
all are sinners, and are unable to comply with its

requirements. No matter how diligently nor how
zealously a man works, nothing that he can do will
meet the full measure of the law's demands. It is
too high for him to attain to; he cannot obtain
righteousness by the law. "By the deeds of the
law there shall no flesh be justified [made righteous]
in His sight." What a deplorable condition! We
must have the righteousness of the law or we cannot enter heaven, and yet the law has no righteousness for one of us. It will not yield to our most
persistent and energetic efforts the smallest portion
of that holiness without which no man can see the
Lord.

Who, then, can be saved? Can there, then, be such
a thing as a righteous person?—Yes, for the Bible
often speaks of them. It speaks of Lot as "that
righteous man;" it says, "Say ye to the righteous,
that it shall be well with him; for they shall eat
the fruit of their doings" (Isa. 3: 10), thus indicat-
ing that there will be righteous persons to receive
the reward; and it plainly declares that there will
be a righteous nation at the last, saying: "In that
day shall this song be sung in the land of Judah:
We have a strong city; salvation will God appoint
for walls and bulwarks. Open ye the gates, that
the righteous nation which keepeth the truth may
enter in." Isa. 26: 1, 2. David says, "Thy law is
the truth." Ps. 119: 142. It is not only truth,
but it is the sum of all truth; consequently the nation that keeps the truth will be a nation that keeps

the law of God. Such will be doers of His will, and they shall enter into the kingdom of heaven. Matt. 7 : 21.

THE LORD OUR RIGHTEOUSNESS.

The question, then, is, How may the righteousness that is necessary in order that one may enter that city, be obtained? To answer this question is the great work of the Gospel. Let us first have an object lesson on justification, or the imparting of righteousness. The fact may help us to a better understanding of the theory. The example is given in Luke 18 : 9–14, in these words:—

"And He spake this parable unto certain which trusted in themselves that they were righteous, and despised others: Two men went up into the temple to pray; the one a Pharisee, and the other a publican. The Pharisee stood and prayed thus with himself, God, I thank thee, that I am not as other men are, extortioners, unjust, adulterers, or even as this publican. I fast twice in the week, I give tithes of all that I possess. And the publican, standing afar off, would not lift up so much as his eyes unto heaven, but smote upon his breast, saying, God be merciful to me a sinner. I tell you, this man went down to his house justified rather than the other; for everyone that exalteth himself shall be abased; and he that humbleth himself shall be exalted."

This was given to show how we may not, and how we may, attain to righteousness. The Pharisees are not extinct; there are many in these days who expect to gain righteousness by their own good deeds. They trust in themselves that they are righteous. They do not always so openly boast of their goodness, but they show in other ways that they are trusting to their own righteousness. Perhaps the spirit of the Pharisee—the spirit which would recount to God one's own good deeds as a reason for favor—is found as frequently as anywhere else among those professed Christians who feel the most bowed down on account of their sins. They know that they have sinned, and they feel condemned. They mourn over their sinful state, and deplore their weakness. Their testimonies never rise above this level. Often they refrain for very shame from speaking in the social meeting, and often they do not dare approach God in prayer. After having sinned to a greater degree than usual, they refrain from prayer for some time, until the vivid sense of their failure has passed away, or until they imagine that they have made up for it by special good behavior. Of what is this a manifestation ?—Of that Pharisaic spirit that would flaunt its own righteousness in the face of God; that will not come before Him unless it can lean on the false prop of its own fancied goodness. They want to be able to say to the Lord, " See how good I have been for the past few days; you surely will accept me now."

But what is the result ?—The man who trusted in his own righteousness had none, while the man who prayed, in heart-felt contrition, "God be merciful to me, a sinner," went down to his house a righteous man. Christ says that he went *justified*, that is, made righteous.

Notice that the publican did something more than bewail his sinfulness; he asked for mercy. What is mercy?—It is unmerited favor. It is the disposition to treat a man better than he deserves. Now the Word of Inspiration says of God: "As the heaven is high above the earth, so great is His mercy toward them that fear Him." Ps. 103:11. That is, the measure by which God treats us better than we deserve when we humbly come to Him, is the distance between earth and the highest heaven. And in what respect does He treat us better than we deserve?—In taking our sins away from us; for the next verse says: "As far as the east is from the west, so far hath He removed our transgressions from us." With this agree the words of the beloved disciple: "If we confess our sins, He is faithful and just to forgive us our sins, and to cleanse us from all unrighteousness." 1 John 1:9.

For a further statement of the mercy of God, and of how it is manifested, read Micah 7:18, 19: "Who is a god like unto Thee, that pardoneth iniquity, and passeth by the transgression of the remnant of His heritage? He retaineth not His anger forever, because He delighteth in mercy. He will turn again, He will have compassion upon us; He will subdue our iniquities; and Thou wilt cast all their sins into the depths of the sea." Let us now read the direct Scripture statement of how righteousness is bestowed.

The apostle Paul, having proved that all have

sinned and come short of the glory of God, so that
by the deeds of the law no flesh shall be justified in
his sight, proceeds to say that we are "justified
[made righteous] freely by his grace through the
redemption that is in Christ Jesus; whom God hath
set forth to be a propitiation through faith in His
blood, to declare His righteousness for the remission
of sins that are past, through the forbearance of
God; to declare, I say, at this time His righteousness; that He might be just, and the justifier of Him
that believeth in Jesus." Rom. 3:24–26.

"Being made righteous freely." How else could
it be? Since the best efforts of a sinful man have
not the least effect toward producing righteousness,
it is evident that the only way it can come to him
is as a gift. That righteousness is a gift is plainly
stated by Paul in Rom. 5: 17 : " For if by one man's
offense death reigned by one; much more they
which receive abundance of grace and of the gift
of righteousness shall reign in life by One, Jesus
Christ." It is because righteousness is a gift that
eternal life, which is the reward of righteousness, is
the gift of God, through Jesus Christ our Lord.

Christ has been set forth by God as the One
through whom forgiveness of sins is to be obtained;
and this forgiveness consists simply in the declaration of His righteousness (which is the righteousness
of God) for their remission. God, "who is rich in
mercy" (Eph. 2 : 4), and who delights in it, puts His
own righteousness on the sinner who believes in

Jesus, as a substitute for his sins. Surely, this is a profitable exchange for the sinner, and it is no loss to God, for He is infinite in holiness, and the supply can never be diminished.

The scripture that we have just been considering (Rom. 3:24–26) is but another statement of verses 21, 22, following the declaration that by the deeds of the law there shall no flesh be made righteous. The apostle adds: "But now the righteousness of God without the law is manifested, being witnessed by the law and the prophets; even the righteousness of God which is by faith of Jesus Christ unto all and upon all them that believe." God puts His righteousness upon the believer. He covers him with it, so that his sin no more appears. Then the forgiven one can exclaim with the prophet:—

"I will greatly rejoice in the Lord, my soul shall be joyful in my God; for He hath clothed me with the garments of salvation, He hath covered me with the robe of righteousness, as a bridegroom decketh himself with ornaments, and as a bride adorneth herself with her jewels." Isa. 61:10.

But what about "the righteousness of God without the law"? How does that accord with the statement that the law is the righteousness of God, and that outside of its requirements there is no righteousness? There is no contradiction here. The law is not ignored by this process. Note carefully: Who gave the law?—Christ. How did He speak it?—"As one having authority," even as God. The law sprang from Him the same as from the

Father, and is simply a declaration of the righteousness of His character. Therefore the righteousness which comes by the faith of Jesus Christ is the same righteousness that is epitomized in the law; and this is further proved by the fact that it is "witnessed by the law."

Let the reader try to picture the scene. Here stands the law as the swift witness against the sinner. It cannot change, and it will not call a sinner a righteous man. The convicted sinner tries again and again to obtain righteousness from the law, but it resists all his advances. It cannot be bribed by any amount of penance or professedly good deeds. But here stands Christ, "full of grace" as well as of truth, calling the sinner to Him. At last the sinner, weary of the vain struggle to get righteousness from the law, listens to the voice of Christ, and flees to His outstretched arms. Hiding in Christ, he is covered with His righteousness; and now behold! he has obtained, through faith in Christ, that for which he has been vainly striving. He has the righteousness which the law requires, and it is the genuine article, because he obtained it from the Source of Righteousness; from the very place whence the law came. And the law witnesses to the genuineness of this righteousness. It says that so long as the man retains that, it will go into court and defend him against all accusers. It will witness to the fact that he is a righteous man. With the righteousness which is "through the faith of Christ, the righteousness which is of God by faith " (Phil. 3:9), Paul was sure that he would stand secure in the day of Christ.

There is in the transaction no ground for finding fault. God is just, and at the same time the Justifier of him that believeth in Jesus. In Jesus dwells all the fullness of the Godhead; He is equal with the Father in every attribute. Consequently the redemption that is in Him—the ability to buy back lost man—is infinite. Man's rebellion is against the Son as much as against the Father, since both are one. Therefore, when Christ "gave Himself for our sins," it was the King suffering for the rebellious subjects—the One injured passing by, overlooking, the offense of the offender. No skeptic will deny that any man has the right and privilege of pardoning any offense committed against himself; then why cavil when God exercises the same right? Surely if He wishes to pardon the injury done Himself, He has the right; and more because He vindicates the integrity of His law, by submitting in His own Person to the penalty which was due the sinner. "But the innocent suffered for the guilty." True; but the innocent Sufferer "gave Himself" voluntarily, in order that He might in justice to His government do what His love prompted, namely, pass by the injury done to Himself as the Ruler of the universe.

Now read God's own statement of His own Name —a statement given in the face of one of the worst cases of contempt ever shown Him:—

"And the Lord descended in the cloud, and stood with him there, and proclaimed the Name of the Lord. And the Lord passed by before him, and proclaimed, The Lord, The Lord God, merciful and gracious, long-suffering, and abundant in goodness and truth, keeping mercy for thousands, forgiving iniquity and transgression and sin, and that will by no means clear the guilty." Ex. 34 : 5–7.

This is God's Name; it is the character in which He reveals Himself to man; the light in which He wishes men to regard Him. But what of the declaration that He " will by no means clear the guilty"? That is perfectly in keeping with His long-suffering, abundant goodness, and His passing by the transgression of His people. It is true that God will by no means clear the guilty; He could not do that and still be a just God. But He does something which is far better: *he removes the guilt*, so that the one formerly guilty does not need to be cleared,— he is justified, and counted as though he never had sinned.

Let no one cavil over the expression, " putting on righteousness," as though such a thing were hypocrisy. Some, with a singular lack of appreciation of the value of the gift of righteousness, have said that they did not want righteousness that was " put on," but that they wanted only that righteousness which comes from the life, thus depreciating the righteousness of God, which is by faith of Jesus Christ *unto* all and *upon* all that believe. We agree with their idea in so far as it is a protest against hypocrisy, a form of godliness without the power;

but we would have the reader bear this thought in mind: It makes a vast deal of difference who puts *the righteousness on.* If we attempt to put it on ourselves, then we really get on nothing but a filthy garment, no matter how beautiful it may look to us; but when Christ clothes us with it, it is not to be despised nor rejected. Mark the expression in Isaiah: "He hath covered me with the robe of righteousness." The righteousness with which Christ covers us is righteousness that meets the approval of God; and if God is satisfied with it, surely men ought not to try to find anything better.

But we will carry the figure a step further, and that will relieve the matter of all difficulty. Zech. 3:1-5 furnishes the solution; it reads thus:—

"And he showed me Joshua the high priest standing before the Angel of the Lord, and Satan standing at His right hand to resist Him. And the Lord said unto Satan, The Lord rebuke thee, O Satan; even the Lord that hath chosen Jerusalem rebuke thee; is not this a brand plucked out of the fire? Now Joshua was clothed with filthy garments, and stood before the Angel. And He answered and spake unto those that stood before Him, saying, Take away the filthy garments from him. And unto him He said, Behold, I have caused thine iniquity to pass from thee, and I will clothe thee with change of raiment. And I said, Let them set a fair miter upon his head. So they set a fair miter upon his head, and clothed him with garments. And the Angel of the Lord stood by."

Notice in the above account that the taking away of the filthy garments is the same as causing the iniquity to pass from the person. And so we find that when Christ covers us with the robe of His own righteousness, He does not furnish a cloak for sin, but takes the sin away.   And this shows that the forgiveness of sins is something more than a mere form, something more than a mere entry in the books of record in heaven, to the effect that the sin has been canceled.   The forgiveness of sins is a reality; it is something tangible, something that vitally affects the individual.   It actually clears him from guilt; and if he is cleared from guilt, is justified, made righteous, he has certainly undergone a radical change.   He is, indeed, another person.   For he obtained this righteousness for the remission of sins, in Christ.   It was obtained only by putting on Christ.   But "if any man be in Christ, he is a new creature."   2 Cor. 5:17.   And so the full and free forgiveness of sins carries with it that wonderful and miraculous change known as the new birth; for a man cannot become a new creature except by a new birth.   This is the same as having a new, or a clean, heart.

The new heart is a heart that loves righteousness and hates sin.   It is a heart of willingness to be led into the paths of righteousness.   It is such a heart as the Lord wished Israel to have when he said, "O that there were such a heart in them, that they would fear Me, and keep all My commandments always, that it might be well with them, and with their children forever!"   Deut. 5 : 29.   In short, it is a heart free from the love of sin as well as from the guilt of sin. But what makes a man sincerely desire the forgiveness of his sins?—It is simply his hatred of them, and his desire for righteousness, which hatred and desire have been enkindled by the Holy Spirit.

The Spirit strives with all men. It comes as a reprover; when its voice of reproof is regarded, then it at once assumes the office of comforter. The same submissive, yielding disposition that leads the person to accept the reproof of the Spirit, will also lead him to follow the teachings of the Spirit, and Paul says that "as many as are led by the Spirit of God, they are the sons of God." Rom. 8: 14.

Again, what brings justification, or the forgiveness of sins? It is faith, for Paul says: "Therefore being justified by faith, we have peace with God through our Lord Jesus Christ." Rom. 5: 1. The righteousness of God is given unto and put upon everyone that believeth. Rom. 3: 22. But this same exercise of faith makes the person a child of God; for, says the apostle Paul again, "Ye are all the children of God by faith in Christ Jesus." Gal. 3: 26.

The fact that everyone whose sins are forgiven is at once a child of God, is shown in Paul's letter to Titus. He first brings to view the wicked condition in which we once were, and then says (Titus 3: 4–7):—

" But after that the kindness and love of God our Saviour

toward men appeared, not by works of righteousness which we have done, but according to His mercy He saved us, by the washing of regeneration, and renewing of the Holy Ghost; which He shed on us abundantly through Jesus Christ our Saviour ; that being justified by His grace, we should be made heirs according to the hope of eternal life.''

Note that it is by being justified by His grace that we are made heirs.   We have already learned from Rom. 3:24, 25 that this justification by his grace is through our faith in Christ; but Gal. 3:26 tells us that faith in Christ Jesus makes us children of God; therefore we know that whoever has been justified by God's grace,—has been forgiven,—is a child and an heir of God.

This shows that there is no ground for the idea that a person must go through a sort of probation, and attain to a certain degree of holiness, before God will accept Him as His child.   He receives us just as we are.   It is not for our goodness that He loves us, but because of our need.   He receives us, not for the sake of anything that He sees in us, but for His own sake, and for what He knows that His Divine power can make of us.   It is only when we realize the wonderful exaltation and holiness of God, and the fact that He comes to us, in our sinful and degraded condition, to adopt us into His family, that we can appreciate the force of the apostle's exclamation, "Behold, what manner of love the Father hath bestowed upon us, that we should be called the sons of God."   1 John 3:1. Everyone upon whom this honor has been bestowed, will purify himself, even as He is pure.

God does not adopt us as His children because we are good, but in order that He may make us good. Says Paul: "God, who is rich in mercy, for His great love wherewith He loved us, even when we were dead in sins, hath quickened us [made us alive] together with Christ (by grace ye are saved), and hath raised us up together, and made us sit together in heavenly places in Christ Jesus; that in the ages to come He might show the exceeding riches of His grace in His kindness toward us through Christ Jesus." Eph. 2:4–7. And then he adds: "For by grace are ye saved through faith; and that not of yourselves; it is the gift of God; not of works, lest any man should boast. For we are His workmanship, created in Christ Jesus unto good works, which God hath before ordained that we should walk in them." Verses 8–10. This passage shows that God loved us while we were yet dead in sins; He gives us His Spirit to make us alive in Christ, and the same Spirit marks our adoption into the Divine family; and He thus adopts us that, as new creatures in Christ, we may do the good works which God has ordained.

ACCEPTANCE WITH GOD.

Many people hesitate to make a start to serve the Lord, because they fear that God will not accept them; and thousands who have been professed followers of Christ for years are still doubting their acceptance with God. For the benefit of such I write, and I would not bewilder their minds with speculations, but will endeavor to give them the simple assurances of God's word.

"Will the Lord receive me?" I reply by another question: Will a man receive that which he has bought? If you go to the store and make a purchase, will you receive the goods when they are delivered? Of course you will; there is no room for any question about it. The fact that you bought the goods, and paid your money for them, is sufficient proof, not only that you are *willing*, but that you are *anxious*, to receive them. If you did not want them, you would not have bought them. Moreover, the more you paid for them the more anxious you are to receive them. If the price that you paid was great, and you had almost given your life to earn it, then there can be no question but that you will accept the purchase when it is delivered. Your great anxiety is lest there should be some failure to deliver it.

Now let us apply this simple, natural illustration to the case of the sinner coming to Christ. In the first place, He has bought us. "What? know ye not that your body is the temple of the Holy Ghost which is in you, which ye have of God, and ye are not your own? For ye are bought with a price." 1 Cor. 6: 19, 20.

The price that was paid for us was His own blood —His life. Paul said to the elders of Ephesus: "Take heed therefore unto yourselves, and to all the

flock, over the which the Holy Ghost hath made
you overseers, to feed the church of God, which He
hath purchased with His own blood." Acts 20:28.
"For as much as ye know that ye were not re-
deemed with corruptible things, as silver and gold,
from your vain conversation [manner of life] received
by tradition from your fathers; but with the precious blood of Christ, as of a lamb without blem-
ish and without spot." 1 Peter 1:18, 19. He
"gave Himself for us." Titus 2:14. He "gave
Himself for our sins, that He might deliver us
from this present evil world, according to the
will of God and our Father." Gal. 1:4.

He bought not a certain class, but the whole
world of sinners. "For God so loved *the world*,
that He gave His only-begotten Son." John 3:16.
Jesus said, "The bread that I will give is My flesh,
which I will give for the life of the world." John
6:51. "For when we were yet without strength,
in due time Christ died for the ungodly." "God
commendeth His love toward us, in that, while we
were yet sinners, Christ died for us." Rom. 5:6, 8.

The price paid was infinite, therefore we know
that He very much desired that which He bought.
He had His heart set on obtaining it. He could not
be satisfied without it. See Phil. 2:6–8; Heb.
12:2; Isa. 53:11.

"But I am not worthy." That means that you are
are not worth the price paid, and therefore you fear
to come lest Christ will repudiate the purchase.

Now you might have some fear on that score if the bargain were not sealed, and the price were not already paid. If He should refuse to accept you, on the ground that you are not worth the price, He would not only lose you, but also the amount paid. Even though the goods for which you have paid are not worth what you gave for them, you yourself would not be so foolish as to throw them away. You would rather get some return for your money than get nothing.

But, further, you have nothing to do with the question of worth. When Christ was on earth in the interest of the purchase, He "needed not that any should testify of man; for He knew what was in man." John 2:25. He made the purchase with his eyes open, and He knew the exact value of that which He bought. He is not at all disappointed when you come to Him and He finds that you are worthless. You have not to worry over the question of worth; if He, with His perfect knowledge of the case, was satisfied to make the bargain, you should be the last one to complain.

For, most wonderful truth of all, He bought you for the very reason that you were not worthy. His practiced eye saw in you great possibilities, and He bought you, not for what you were then or are now worth, but for what He could make of you. He says: "I, even I, am He that blotteth out thy transgressions for Mine own sake." Isa. 43:25. We have no righteousness, therefore He bought us, "that

we might be made the righteousness of God in Him."
Says Paul: "For in Him dwelleth all the fullness of
the Godhead bodily. And ye are complete in Him,
which is the head of all principality and power."
Col. 2:9, 10. Here is the whole process:—

"We all . . . were by nature the children of wrath,
even as others. But God, who is rich in mercy, for His
great love wherewith He loved us, even when we were dead
in sins, hath quickened us together with Christ (by grace ye
are saved), and hath raised us up together, and made us sit
together in heavenly places in Christ Jesus; that in the ages
to come He might show the exceeding riches of His grace in
His kindness toward us through Christ Jesus. For by grace
are ye saved through faith; and that not of yourselves; it is
the gift of God; not of works, lest any man should boast.
For we are His workmanship, created in Christ Jesus unto
good works, which God hath before ordained that we should
walk in them." Eph. 1:3-10.

We are to be "to the praise of the glory of His
grace." This we could not be if we were originally
worth all He paid for us. There would in that case
be no glory to Him in the transaction. He could
not, in the ages to come, show in us the riches of
His grace. But when He takes us, worth nothing,
and at the last presents us faultless before the
throne, it will be to His everlasting glory. And
then there will not be any to ascribe worthiness to
themselves. Throughout eternity, the sanctified
hosts will unite in saying to Christ: "Thou art
worthy . . . for Thou wast slain, and hast re-
deemed us to God by Thy blood out of every kin-
dred, and tongue, and people, and nation; and hast

made us unto our God kings and priests." "Worthy is the Lamb that was slain to receive power, and riches, and wisdom, and strength, and honor, and glory, and blessing." Rev. 5:9, 10, 12.

Surely all doubt as to acceptance with God ought to be set at rest. But it is not. The evil heart of unbelief still suggests doubts. "I believe all this, but—." There, stop right there; if you believed you wouldn't say "but.' When people add "but" to the statement that they believe, they really mean, "I believe, but I don't believe." But you continue: "Perhaps you are right, but hear me out. What I was going to say is, I believe the Scripture statements that you have quoted, but the Bible says that if we are children of God we shall have the witness of the Spirit, and will have the witness in ourselves; and I don't feel any such witness, therefore I *can't* believe that I am Christ's. I believe His word, but I haven't the witness." I understand your difficulty; let me see if it cannot be removed.

As to your being Christ's, you yourself can settle that. You have seen what He gave for you. Now the question is, Have you delivered yourself to Him? If you have, you may be sure that He has accepted you. If you are not His, it is solely because you have refused to deliver to Him that which He has bought. You are defrauding Him. He says, "All day long I have stretched forth My hands unto a disobedient and gainsaying people." Rom. 10:21. He begs you to give Him that

which He has bought and paid for, yet you refuse,
and charge Him with not being willing to receive
you. But if from the heart you have yielded
yourself to Him to be His child, you may be assured
that He has received you.

Now as to your believing His words, yet doubting if He accepts you, because you don't feel the
witness in your heart, I still insist that you don't
believe. If you did, you would have the witness.
Listen to His word: " He that believeth on the Son
of God hath the witness in himself; he that believeth not God hath made Him a liar, because he believeth not the record that God gave of His Son."
1 John 5: 10. To believe in the Son is simply to
believe His word and the record concerning Him.

And "*he that believeth on the Son of God hath the
witness in himself.*" You can't have the witness
until you believe; and as soon as you do believe,
you have the witness. How is that? Because
your belief in God's word is the witness. God says
so: " Now *faith is the substance* of things hoped
for, *the evidence* of things not seen." Heb. 11:1.

If you should hear God say with an audible
voice that you are His child, you would consider
that sufficient witness. Well, when God speaks in
His word, it is the same as though He spoke with
an audible voice; and your faith is the evidence
that you hear and believe.

This is so important a matter that it is worth
careful consideration. Let us read a little more of

the record. First, we read that we are "all the children of God by faith in Christ Jesus." Gal. 3:26. This is a positive confirmation of what I said concerning our unbelief in the witness. Our faith makes us children of God. But how do we obtain this faith?—"Faith cometh by hearing, and hearing by the word of God." Rom. 10:17. But how can we obtain faith in God's word?—Just believe that God cannot lie. You would hardly call God a liar to His face; but that is just what you do if you don't believe His word. All you have to do to believe is to *believe.* "The word is nigh thee, even in thy mouth, and in thy heart; that is, the word of faith, which we preach; that if thou shalt confess with thy mouth the Lord Jesus, and shalt believe in thine heart that God hath raised Him from the dead, thou shalt be saved. For with the heart man believeth unto righteousness; an ' with the mouth confession is made unto salvation. For the Scripture saith, Whosoever believeth on Him shall not be ashamed." Rom. 10:8–11.

All this is in harmony with the record given through Paul: "The Spirit Itself beareth witness with our spirit, that we are the children of God; and if children, then heirs; heirs of God, and joint heirs with Christ." Rom. 8:16, 17. This Spirit which witnesses with our spirit is the Comforter that Jesus promised. John 14:16. And we know that Its witness is true, for It is the "Spirit of truth." Now how does It bear witness?—By bringing to our remembrance the Word which has been recorded. It inspired those words (1 Cor. 2:13; 2 Peter 1:21), and, therefore, when It brings them to our remembrance, it is the same as though It were speaking them directly to us. It presents to our mind the record, part of which we have quoted; we know that the record is true, for God cannot lie; we bid Satan be gone with his false witness against God, and we believe that record; but if we believe the record, we know that we are children of God, and we cry, "Abba, Father." And then the glorious truth breaks more fully upon the soul. The repetition of the words makes it a reality to us. He is *our Father;* we are His children. What joy the thought gives! So we see that the witness which we have in ourselves is not a simple impression, or an emotion. God does not ask us to trust so unreliable a witness as our feeling. He who trusts his own heart is a fool, the Scripture says. But the witness that we are to trust is the unchangeable word of God, and this witness we may have through the Spirit, in our own hearts. "Thanks be unto God for His unspeakable Gift."

This assurance does not warrant us in relaxing our diligence and settling down contentedly, as though we had gained perfection. We must remember that Christ accepts us not for our sake, but for His own sake; not because we are perfect, but that in Him we may go on unto perfection. He blesses us, not because we have been so good that we have deserved a blessing, but in order that in the strength of the blessing we may turn away from our iniquities. Acts 3:26. To everyone that believes in Christ, the power—right or privilege—is given to become the sons of God. John 1:12, margin. It is by the "exceeding great and precious promises" of God through Christ that we are "made partakers of the Divine nature." 2 Peter 1:4.

Let us consider briefly the practical application of some of these scriptures.

THE VICTORY OF FAITH.

The Bible says that "the just shall live by faith." The righteousness of God is "revealed from faith to faith." Rom. 1:17. Nothing can better illustrate the working of faith than some of the examples that are recorded for our learning, "that we through patience and comfort of the Scriptures might have hope." Rom. 15:4. We will take, first, a notable event recorded in the twentieth chapter of 2 Chronicles. Let the reader follow the running comment with his Bible.

"It came to pass after this, also, that the children of Moab, and the children of Ammon and with them other beside the Ammonites, came against Jehoshaphat to battle. Then there came some that told Jehoshaphat, saying, There cometh a great multitude against thee from beyond the sea on this side Syria; and, behold, they be in Hazazon-tamar, which is Engedi." Verses 1, 2.

This great host caused the king and the people to fear, but they took the wise course of gathering together, "to ask help of the Lord; even out of all the cities of Judah they came to seek the Lord." Verses 3, 4. Then follows the prayer of Jehoshaphat, as leader of the congregation, and it is worth special study, since it was a prayer of faith, and contained within itself the beginning of victory:—

"And Jehoshaphat stood in the congregation of Judah and Jerusalem, in the house of the Lord, before the new court, and said, O Lord God of our fathers, art not Thou God in heaven? and rulest Thou not over all the kingdoms of the heathen? and in Thine hand is there not power and might, so that none is able to withstand Thee?" Verses 5, 6.

That was an excellent beginning of a prayer. It starts with a recognition of God in heaven. So the model prayer begins, "Our Father who art in heaven." What does this signify?—That God, as God in heaven, is Creator. It carries with it the recognition of His power over all the kingdoms of the world and of the powers of darkness; the fact that He is in heaven, the Creator, shows that in His hand there is power and might, so that none is able to withstand Him. Why, the man who can begin his prayer in the hour of need with such a recognition of God's power, has victory already on his side. For, notice, Jehoshaphat not only declared his faith in God's wondrous power, but he claimed God's strength as his own, saying, "Art not Thou *our God?* He fulfilled the Scripture requirement: "He that cometh to God must believe

that He is, and that He is a rewarder of them
that diligently seek Him."

Jehoshaphat then proceeded to recount how the
Lord had established them in that land, and how,
although he had not suffered them to invade
Moab and Ammon, those nations had come to cast
them out of their God-given inheritance.   Verses
7–11.   And then he concluded: " O our God, wilt
Thou not judge them? for we have no might against
this great company that cometh against us; neither
know we what to do; but our eyes are upon Thee."
Verse 12.   It is nothing with the Lord to help,
whether with many, or with them that have no
power (2 Chron. 14:11); and since the eyes of the
Lord run to and fro throughout the earth to show
Himself strong in the behalf of those whose heart
is entire towards Him (2 Chron. 16:9), it well becomes those who are in need, to trust Him alone.
This position of Jehoshaphat and his people was in
keeping with the apostolic injunction, " Looking
unto Jesus the Author and Finisher of our faith."
Heb. 12:2.   He is the beginning and the end, and
all power in heaven and earth is in His hands.

Now, what was the result?—The prophet of the
Lord came in the power of the Holy Spirit, " and
he said, Hearken ye, all Judah, and ye inhabitants
of Jerusalem, and thou King Jehoshaphat, Thus
saith the Lord unto you, Be not afraid nor dis-
mayed by reason of this great multitude; for the
battle is not yours, but God's."   Verse 15.   And

then came the command to go forth in the morning to meet the enemy, and they should see the salvation of the Lord, for He would be with them.

Now comes the most important part:—

"And they rose early in the morning, and went forth into the wilderness of Tekoa; and as they went forth, Jehosha· phat stood and said, Hear me, O Judah, and ye inhabitants of Jerusalem: Believe in the Lord your God, so shall ye be established; believe His prophets, so shall ye prosper. And when he had consulted with the people, he appointed singers unto the Lord, and that should praise the beauty of holiness, as they went out before the army, and to say, Praise the Lord; for His mercy endureth forever." Verses 20, 21.

Surely, this was a strange way to go out to battle. Few armies have ever gone to battle with such a vanguard. But what was the result?

"And when they began to sing and to praise, the Lord set ambushments against the children of Ammon, Moab, and Mount Seir, which were come against Judah; and they were smitten. For the children of Ammon and Moab stood up against the inhabitants of Mount Seir, utterly to slay and destroy them; and when they had made an end of the inhabitants of Seir, everyone helped to destroy another. And when Judah came toward the watch-tower in the wilderness, they looked unto the multitude, and, behold, they were dead bodies fallen to the earth, and none escaped." Verses 22–24.

If there have been few armies that have gone to battle with such a vanguard as did the army of Jehoshaphat, it is equally certain that few armies have been rewarded by such a signal victory. And it may not be amiss to study a little into the philosophy of the victory of faith, as illustrated in this instance. When the enemy, who had been confident in their superior numbers, heard the Israelites coming out that morning, singing and shouting, what must they have concluded?—Nothing else but that the Israelites had received re-inforcements, and were so strengthened that it would be useless to try to oppose them. So a panic seized them, and each one looked upon his neighbor as an enemy.

And were they not correct in their conclusion, that Israel had received re-inforcements?—Indeed they were; for the record says: "When they began to sing and to praise, *the Lord set ambushments* against the children of Ammon, Moab, and Mount Seir." The host of the Lord, in whom Jehoshaphat and his people trusted, fought for them. They had re-inforcements, and doubtless if their eyes could have been opened to see them, they would have seen, as did the servant of Elisha on one occasion, that they that were with them were more in number than the enemy.

But the point which should be specially noticed is that it was when Israel began to sing and to praise that the Lord set ambushments against the enemy. What does that signify?—It signifies that their faith was real. The promise of God was considered as good as the actual accomplishment. So they believed in the Lord, or, more literally, they built upon the Lord, and thus they were established, or built up. Thus they proved the truth of the words, "This is the victory that overcometh the world, even our faith." 1 John 5:4.

Let us now apply this illustration in a case of conflict against sin. Here comes a strong temptation to do a thing known to be wrong. We have often proved to our sorrow the strength of the temptation, because it has vanquished us, so that we know that we have no might against it. But now our eyes are upon the Lord, who has told us to come with boldness to the throne of grace, that we may obtain mercy and find grace to help in time of need. So we begin to pray to God for help. And we pray to the God that is revealed to us in the Bible as the Creator of heaven and earth. We begin, not with a mournful statement of our weakness, but with a joyful acknowledgment of God's mighty power. That being settled, we can venture to state our difficulty and our weakness. If we state our weakness first, and our discouraging situation, we are placing ourselves before God. In that case Satan will magnify the difficulty and throw his darkness around us so that we can see nothing else but our weakness, and so, although our cries and pleading may be fervent and agonizing, they will be in vain, because they will lack the essential element of believing that God is, and that He is all that He has revealed Himself to be. But when we start with a recognition of God's power, then we can safely state our weakness, for then we are simply placing our weakness by the side of His power, and the contrast tends to beget courage.

Then, as we pray, the promise of God comes to

our mind, brought there by the Holy Spirit. It may be that we can think of no special promise that exactly fits the case; but we can remember that " this is a faithful saying, and worthy of all acceptation, that Christ Jesus came into the world to save sinners" (1 Tim. 1 : 15); and that He " gave Himself for our sins, that He might deliver us from this present evil world, according to the will of God and our Father" (Gal. 1 : 4); and we may know that this carried with it every promise, for " He that spared not his own Son, but delivered Him up for us all, how shall He not with Him also freely give us all things?" Rom. 8 : 32.

Then we remember that God can speak of those things that are not as though they were. That is if God gives a promise, it is as good as fulfilled already. And so, knowing that our deliverance from evil is according to the will of God (Gal. 1 : 4), we count the victory as already ours, and begin to thank God for His " exceeding great and precious promises." As our faith grasps these promises and makes them real, we cannot help praising God for His wonderful love; and while we are doing this, our minds are wholly taken from evil, and the victory is ours. The Lord sets ambushments against the enemy. Our ascription of praise shows to Satan that we have obtained re-inforcements; and as he has tested the power of the help that is granted to us, he knows that he can do nothing on that occasion, and so he leaves us. This illustrates the force of the apostle's injunction:—

"Be careful for nothing [that is, do not worry about any-thing]; but in everything by prayer and supplication *with thanksgiving* let your requests be made known unto God." Phil. 4: 6.

BOND-SERVANTS AND FREEMEN.

The power of faith in bringing victory may be shown by another line of Scripture texts, which are exceedingly practical. In the first place, let it be understood that the sinner is a slave. Christ said: "Whosoever committeth sin is the servant of sin." John 8: 34. Paul also says, putting himself in the place of an unrenewed man: "For we know that the law is spiritual; but I am carnal, sold under sin." Rom. 7: 14. A man who is sold is a slave; therefore the man who is sold under sin is the slave of sin. Peter brings to view the same fact, when, speaking of corrupt, false teachers, he says: "While they promise them liberty, they themselves are the servants of corruption; for of whom a man is over-come, of the same is he brought in bondage." 2 Peter 2: 19.

The prominent characteristic of the slave is that he cannot do as he pleases, but is bound to perform the will of another, no matter how irksome it may be. Paul thus proves the truth of his saying that he, as a carnal man, was the slave of sin: "For that which I do I allow not; for what I would, that do I not; but what I hate, that do I." "Now then it is no more I that do it, but sin that dwelleth in me. For I know that in me (that is, in my flesh) dwelleth no good thing; for to will is present with me; but how to perform that which is good I find not. For the good that I would I do not; but the evil which I would not, that I do." Rom. 7 : 15, 17–19.

The fact that sin controls, proves that a man is a slave; and although everyone that committeth sin is the bond-servant of sin, the slavery becomes unendurable when the sinner has had a glimpse of freedom, and longs for it, yet cannot break the chains which bind him to sin. The impossibility for the unrenewed man to do even the good that he would like to do has been shown already from Rom. 8 : 7, 8 and Gal. 5 : 17.

How many people have in their own experience proved the truth of these scriptures. How many have resolved, and resolved again, and yet their sincerest resolutions have proved in the face of temptation as weak as water. They had no might, and they did not know what to do; and, unfortunately, their eyes were not upon God so much as upon themselves and the enemy. Their experience was one of constant struggle against sin, it is true, but of constant defeat as well.

Call you this a true Christian experience? There are some who imagine that it is. Why, then, did the apostle, in the anguish of his soul, cry out, "O wretched man that I am! who shall deliver me from the body of this death?" Rom. 7 : 24. Is a true Christian experiencing a body of death so terrible that the soul is constrained to cry for deliverance? —Nay, verily.

Again, who is it that, in answer to this earnest appeal, reveals himself as a deliverer?   Says the apostle, " I thank God through Jesus Christ our Lord." In another place he says of Christ:—

"Forasmuch then as the children are partakers of flesh and blood, He also Himself likewise took part of the same; that through death He might destroy him that had the power of death, that is, the devil; and deliver them who through fear of death were all their life-time subject to bondage." Heb. 2 : 14, 15.

Again, Christ thus proclaims His own mission:

"The Spirit of the Lord God is upon Me; because the Lord hath anointed Me to preach good tidings unto the meek; He hath sent Me to bind up the broken-hearted, to proclaim liberty to the captives, and the opening of the prison to them that are bound." Isa. 61: 1.

What this bondage and captivity are has already been shown.   It is the bondage of sin—the slavery of being compelled to sin, even against the will, by the power of inherited and acquired evil propensities and habits.   Does Christ deliver from a true Christian experience?—No, indeed.   Then the bondage of sin, of which the apostle complains in the seventh of Romans, is not the experience of a child of God, but of the servant of sin.   It is to deliver men from this captivity that Christ came; not to deliver us, during this life, from warfare and struggles, but from defeat; to enable us to be strong in the Lord and in the power of His might, so that we could give thanks unto the Father "who hath delivered us from the power of darkness, and hath translated us into the kingdom of His dear Son," through whose blood we have redemption.

How is this deliverance effected?—By the Son of God. Says Christ: " If ye continue in My word, then are ye My disciples indeed; and ye shall know the truth, and the truth shall make you free." "If the Son therefore shall make you free, ye shall be free indeed." John 8 : 31, 32, 36. This freedom comes to everyone that believeth; for to them that believe on His name, He gives the "power to become the sons of God." The freedom from condemnation comes to them who are in Christ Jesus (Rom. 8 : 1); and we put on Christ by faith (Gal. 3 : 26, 27). It is by faith that Christ dwells in our hearts.

PRACTICAL ILLUSTRATIONS OF DELIVERANCE FROM BONDAGE.

Now let us take some illustrations of the power of faith to deliver from bondage. We will quote Luke 13 : 10–17:—

"And He was teaching in one of the synagogues on the Sabbath. And, behold, there was a woman which had a spirit of infirmity eighteen years, and was bowed together, and could in nowise lift up herself. And when Jesus saw her, he called her to Him, and said unto her, Woman, thou art loosed from thine infirmity. And He laid his hands on her; and immediately she was made straight, and glorified God. And the ruler of the synagogue answered with indignation, because that Jesus had healed on the Sabbath-day, and said unto the people, There are six days in which men ought to work; in them therefore come and be healed, and not on the Sabbath-day. The Lord then answered him, and said, Thou hypocrite, doth not each one of you on the

Sabbath loose his ox or his ass from the stall, and lead him away to watering? and ought not this woman, being a daughter of Abraham, whom Satan hath bound, lo, these eighteen years, be loosed from this bond on the Sabbath-day? And when He had said these things, all His adversaries were ashamed; and all the people rejoiced for all the glorious things that were done by Him."

We may pass by the carping of the hypocritical ruler, to consider the miracle. The woman was bound; we, through fear of death, have been all our life-time subject to bondage. Satan had bound the woman; Satan has also set snares for our feet, and has brought us into captivity. She could in nowise lift up herself; our iniquities have taken hold of us, so that we are not able to look up. Ps. 40 : 12. With a word and a touch Jesus set the woman free from her infirmities; we have the same merciful High Priest now in the heavens, who is touched with the feeling of our infirmities, and the same word will deliver us from evil.

For what purpose were the miracles of healing recorded, which were performed by Jesus? John tells us. It was not simply to show that He can heal disease, but to show His power over sin. See Matt. 9 : 2–8. But John says:—

"And many other signs truly did Jesus in the presence of His disciples, which are not written in this book; but these are written, that ye might believe that Jesus is the Christ, the Son of God; and that believing ye might have life through His name." John 20 : 30, 31.

So we see that they are recorded simply as object lessons of Christ's love, of His willingness to

relieve, and of His power over the works of Satan,
no matter whether in the body or in the soul.   One
more miracle must suffice in this connection.   It is
the one recorded in the third chapter of Acts.   I
shall not quote the entire account, but ask the
reader to follow it carefully with his Bible.

Peter and John saw at the gate of the temple
a man over forty years old, who had been lame
from his birth.   He had never walked.   He was
begging, and Peter felt prompted by the Spirit to
give him something better than silver or gold.
Said he: "In the name of Jesus of Nazareth rise
up and walk.   And he took him by the right hand,
and lifted him up, and immediately his feet and
ankle bones received strength.   And he leaping up
stood, and walked, and entered with them into the
temple, walking, and leaping, and praising God."
Verses 6–8.

This notable miracle on one whom all had seen
caused a wonderful excitement among the people;
and when Peter saw their astonishment, he proceeded to tell how the wonder had been performed,
saying:—

"Ye men of Israel, why marvel ye at this? or why look ye
so earnestly on us, as though by our own power or holiness we
had made this man to walk?   The God of Abraham, and of
Isaac, and of Jacob, the God of our fathers, hath glorified
His Son Jesus; whom ye delivered up, . . . and killed
the Prince of Life, whom God hath raised from the dead;
whereof we are witnesses.   *And His Name through faith in
His Name hath made this man strong*, whom ye see and

know; yea, *the faith which is by Him hath given him this perfect soundness* in the presence of you all." Verses 12-16.

Now make the application. "The man was lame
from his mother's womb," unable to help himself.
He would gladly have walked, but he could not.
We likewise can all say, with David, "Behold, I
was shapen in iniquity; and in sin did my mother
conceive me." Ps. 51 : 5. As a consequence, we
are by nature so weak that we cannot do the things
that we would. As each year of the man's life in-
creased his inability to walk, by increasing the
weight of his body, while his limbs grew no
stronger, so the repeated practice of sin, as we grow
older, strengthens its power over us. It was an utter impossibility for that man to walk; yet the Name
of Christ, through faith in it, gave him perfect soundness and freedom from his infirmity. So we, through
the faith which is by Him, may be made whole, and
enabled to do the thing which hitherto has been
impossible. For the things which are impossible
with man are possible with God. He is the Creator. "To them that have no might He increaseth
strength." One of the wonders of faith, as shown
in the cases of the ancient worthies, is that they
"out of weakness were made strong."

By these instances we have seen how God deliv-
ers from bondage those who trust in Him. Now
let us consider the knowledge of how freedom is
maintained.

We have seen that we by nature are all servants

of sin and Satan, and that as soon as we submit to
Christ, we become loosed from Satan's power.   Says
Paul: " Know ye not, that to whom ye yield yourselves servants to obey, his servants ye are to whom
ye obey; whether of sin unto death, or of obedience
unto righteousness?"   Rom. 6: 16.   So then, as
soon as we become free from the bondage of sin,
we become the servants of Christ.   Indeed, the
very act of loosing us from the power of sin, in answer to our faith, proves God's acceptance of us as
His servants.   We become, indeed, the bond-serv-
ants of Christ; but he who is the Lord's servant is
a free man, for we are called unto liberty (Gal. 5:
13), and where the Spirit of the Lord is, there is
liberty (2 Cor. 3: 17).

And now comes the conflict again.   Satan is not
disposed to give up his slave so readily.   He comes,
armed with the lash of fierce temptation, to drive
us again to his service.   We know by sad experience that he is more powerful than we are, and that
unaided we cannot resist him.   But we dread his
power, and cry for help.   Then we call to mind
that we are not Satan's servants any longer.   We
have submitted ourselves to God, and therefore He
accepted us as *His* servants.   So we can say with
the Psalmist, "O Lord, truly I am Thy servant; I
am Thy servant, and the son of Thine handmaid;
Thou hast loosed my bonds."   Ps. 116: 16.   But
the fact that God has loosed the bonds that Satan
had thrown around us—and He has done this if
we believe that He has—is evidence that God will
protect us, for He cares for His own, and we have
the assurance that He that has begun a good work
in us "will perform it until the day of Jesus Christ."
Phil. 1: 6.   And in this confidence we are strong
to resist.

Again, if we have yielded ourselves to be servants of God, we are His servants, or, in other words, are instruments of righteousness in His hands. Read Rom. 6: 13–16. We are not inert, lifeless, senseless instruments, such as the agriculturist uses, which have no voice as to how they shall be used, but living, intelligent instruments, who are permitted to choose their occupation. Nevertheless, the term "instrument" signifies a tool,—something that is entirely under the control of the artisan. The difference between us and the tools of the mechanic is that we can choose who shall use us, and at what kind of service we shall be employed; but having made the choice, and yielded ourselves into the hands of the workman, we are to be as completely in his hands as is the tool, that has no voice as to how it shall be used. When we yield to God, we are to be in His hands as clay in the hands of the potter, that He may do with us as He pleases. Our volition lies in choosing whether or not we will let Him work in us that which is good.

This idea of being instruments in the hands of God is a wonderful aid to the victory of faith when it is once fully grasped. For, notice, what an instrument will do depends entirely upon the person in whose hands it is. Here, for instance, is a die. It is innocent enough in itself, yet it may be used for the basest purposes, as well as for that which is useful. If it be in the hands of a bad character, it may be used in making counterfeit coin. It certainly will not be used for any good purpose. But if it be in the hands of an upright, virtuous man, it cannot possibly do any harm. Likewise, when we were the servants of Satan, we did no good (Rom. 6: 20); but now that we have yielded ourselves into the hands of God, we know that there is no unrighteousness in Him, and so an instrument in His hands cannot be used for an evil purpose. The yielding to God must be as complete as it was formerly to Satan, for the apostle says:—

"I speak after the manner of men because of the infirmity of your flesh; for as ye have yielded your members servants to uncleanness and to iniquity unto iniquity; even so now yield your members servants to righteousness unto holiness." Rom. 6 : 19.

The whole secret of overcoming, then, lies in first wholly yielding to God, with a sincere desire to do His will; next, in knowing that in our yielding He accepts us as His servants; and then, in retaining that submission to Him, and leaving ourselves in His hands. Often victory can be gained only by repeating again and again, *"O Lord, truly I am Thy servant;* I am Thy servant, and the son of Thine handmaid; *Thou hast loosed my bonds."* This is simply an emphatic way of saying, " O Lord, I have yielded myself into Thy hands as an instrument of righteousness; let Thy will be done, and not the dictates of the flesh." But when we can realize the force of that scripture and feel indeed that we are servants of God, immediately will come the thought, " Well, if I am indeed an instrument in the hands of God, He cannot use me to do evil with, nor can He permit me to do evil as long as I remain in His hands. He must keep me if I am kept from evil, because I cannot keep myself. But He wants to keep me from evil, for He has shown His desire, and also His power to fulfill His desire, in giving Himself for me. Therefore I shall be kept from this evil." All these thoughts may pass through the mind instantly; and then with them must necessarily come a feeling of gladness that we shall be kept from the dreaded evil. That gladness naturally finds expression in thanksgiving to God, and while we are thanking God the enemy retires with his temptation, and the peace of God fills the heart. Then we find that the joy in believing far outweighs all the joy that comes from indulgence in sin.

All this is a demonstration of Paul's words: " Do we then make void the law through faith? God forbid; yea, we establish the law." Rom. 3: 31. To " make void" the law is not to abolish it; for no man can abolish the law of God, yet the Psalmist says that it has been made void. Ps. 119: 126. To make void the law of God is something more than to claim that it is of no consequence; it is to show by the life that it is considered of no consequence. A man makes the law of God void when he allows it to have no power in his life. In short, to make void the law of God is to break it; but the law itself remains the same whether it is kept or not. Making it void affects only the individual.

Therefore, when the apostle says that we do not make void the law of God by faith, but that, on the contrary, we establish it, he means that faith does not lead to violation of the law, but to obedience. No, we should not say that faith *leads* to obedience, but that faith itself obeys. Faith establishes the law in the heart. " Faith is the substance of things hoped for." If the thing hoped for be righteousness, faith establishes it. Instead of faith leading to antinomianism, it is the only thing that is contrary to antinomianism. It matters not how much a person boasts in the law of God; if he rejects or ignores implicit faith in Christ, he is in no better state than the man who directly assails the law. The man of faith is the only one who truly honors the law of God. Without faith it is impossible to please God (Heb. 11 : 6); with it, all things are possible (Mark 9 : 23).

Yes, faith does the impossible, and it is just that which God requires us to do. When Joshua said to Israel, " Ye cannot serve the Lord," he told the truth, yet it was a fact that God required them to serve Him. It is not within any man's power to do righteousness, even though he wants to (Gal. 5 : 17); therefore it is a mistake to say that all God wants is for us to do the best we can. He who does no better than that will not do the works of God. No, he must *do better than he can do.* He must do that which only the power of God working through him can do. It is impossible for a man to walk on water, yet Peter did it when he exercised faith in Jesus.

Since all power in heaven and in earth is in the hands of Christ, and this power is at our disposal, even Christ Himself coming to dwell in the heart by faith, there is no room for finding fault with God for requiring us to do the impossible; for " the things which are impossible with men are possible with God." Luke 18 : 27. Therefore we may boldly say, The Lord is my helper, and I will not fear what man shall do unto me." Heb. 13 : 6.

Then " who shall separate us from the love of Christ? shall tribulation, or distress, or persecution, or famine, or nakedness, or peril, or sword? "— " Nay, in all these things we are more than conquerors through Him that loved us." Rom. 8 : 35, 37. "For I am persuaded, that neither death, nor life, nor angels, nor principalities, nor powers, nor things present, nor things to come, nor height, nor depth, nor any other creature, shall be able to separate us from the love of God, which is in Christ Jesus our Lord."